Grounds that our comrade had passed away. Poor Harry was one of the cleverest wing-forwards I have ever known, and he was immensely popular with everybody. He joined the club with me, and with us in the team were McEachrane (now with the Arsenal), Craig (Notts Forest), my partner at full-back, Carnelly, and Joyce. We had some rare talent in our reserve team too, for, if my memory is not at fault, there were J. Bigden (now of the Arsenal), R. Pudan (Bristol Rovers), and Yenson (Queen's Park Rangers).

Retaining several of their old players, in the following season, 1900–1, West Ham finished up sixth on the Southern League table. This, indeed, was progress. It was the first year of the intermediate rounds of the English Cup competition, and it was our fortune to meet Liverpool at the Memorial Grounds. They beat us by only 1 goal, and we were rather unlucky to lose. Goldie (Fulham) played against us, and Satterthwaite, who afterwards became identified with West Ham, was Liverpool's twelfth man. Grassam joined us that year, and Hugh Monteith kept goal for the "Hammers," as we were then styled.

Next season, 1901–2, is the brightest in the history of the club. It was roses all the way, but there was one ugly thorn, and that a beating from Grays United in the National Cup competition. We reached fourth position in the League table, finishing behind Portsmouth, "Spurs," and "Saints."

In that year I was appointed assistant-secretary, and at a later period, as is generally known, I became secretary-manager.

We lost the services of several of our best men the following season, 1902–3. That was the penalty, I suppose, we had to pay for success. All the same, we had a useful team, among whom were Fred Griffiths, the Welsh International goalkeeper; J. Blythe, who afterwards went to Millwall; and Linward, who was transferred to the Arsenal. And the club certainly deserved a higher position than tenth on the table, where we subsequently finished. The Cup competition saw us beaten at Lincoln, and the match will be remembered if only for the accident to Kelly, who, although he broke his ankle, went on playing till within a few minutes of the finish.

Now we come to the season 1903–4. This was one of the most eventful in the history of the club. The West Ham United Football Club Company dates from 1900–1. The open door, so to speak, had been productive of good results. The charge that the club was out of sympathy with the local public was not repeated in 1903. A lot of prejudice had been lived down and forgotten, and I don't suppose any club has had to fight harder for its existence than West Ham United. Even as we stood on the threshold of 1903–4 a great and overwhelming

difficulty beset us. It was the last year of cerning the occupancy of the Memorial Gr

But before I pass along to the stirring the close of that season, let me say something about the team. We were reinforced by a strong contingent from Reading, including Allison, Cotton, Watts, and Lyon. With regard to the performances of the team that year, I regret to say that we did not succeed as we should have liked. Fulham beat us by a goal in the Cup competition, and in the League we were the reverse of comfortable—a fact which did not help to encourage us when we knew that we must leave the Memorial Grounds and that a new home had to be found. The immediate and pressing difficulty of West Ham at the close of the 1904 season was the question of ground. The directors endeavoured to negotiate with Mr. A. F. Hills for a further lease of seven, fourteen, or twenty-one years of the Memorial Grounds at a good rental, the club to have sole control.

Unfortunately as we thought then, but luckily as it afterwards turned out, no agreement could be arrived at. And we had to go. But where to? A piece of waste ground was offered us by the corporation, but this would not do. I well remember the facts concerning our lifting up and being placed on dry land, as it were. It was during our last few days at the Memorial Grounds. A match was being played between boys of the Home Office Schools. One of the Brothers from the Boleyn Castle School was present. We told him of our difficulty, and showed him the letter from Mr. Hills. An arrangement was made with the Brother there and then to go and see the Boleyn Castle Ground. We agreed to take it. A week later we were thrown back into the lap of despair again by being told that the Home Office would not approve of the action of the Brothers. A deputation of directors waited upon Mr. Ernest Gray, M.P., and through his good offices and certain conditions on our part we were finally allowed to take possession of Boleyn Castle.

It is a place with a history. There the unfortunate lady whose name is linked with that of Henry VIII. has resided. There are legends and stories about this fine old mansion—now a school.

At their new ground the West Ham Club hope to make football history, and I may say that 1904–5—our first season at the Castle—was also the first year we have ever made a profit on the season's working.

Before closing I should like to give the names of the present board: Mr. J. Grisdale, chairman; Mr. J. Moss, vice-chairman; Mr. G. C. Fundell, treasurer; Messrs. A. C. Davis, H. Iggulden, W. White, L. Johnson, H. G. Sutton, J. Reeves, and H. Mattocks.

Reeves.]

BOLEYN CASTLE GROUND, THE HISTORIC HOME OF WEST HAM UNITED FOOTBALL CLUB.

It was in the fine old mansion near by, which gave the ground its name, that Anne Boleyn, the unfortunate wife of King Henry VIII., once resided. West Ham United are rapidly making history of another sort here, and it seems that at last the club has embarked upon a flood-tide of prosperity.

1895 - 1995 Hammers 100 Years of Football

THIS book represents a celebration of a century of soccer in London's East End.

From the Victorian endeavours of the early Thames Ironworks pioneers, whose pounding Hammers rang out across the River Thames to give this famous club its unique identity, to the pomp and splendour of the new Bobby Moore South Stand and Centenary Stand, it's all here.

A claret and blue kaleidoscope designed to create a visual picture of a great football club, reflecting the changes in fashion, as well as football, in 100 years of humour, heartbreak and heroes.

As we take our seats in the modern-day, all-seater Upton Park, it's easy to forget the famous old wooden Chicken Run and cramped confines of the Boleyn Ground with its quaint castle on Green Street.

The pages of this book will stir fond memories of past glory days and the players and personalities who established the name West Ham United in football folklore. The somewhat unusual design conveys the different atmospheres engendered by each decade.

This is not an ordinary football book. But then West Ham United is not an ordinary football club.

Published on behalf of West Ham United FC by Independent UK Sports Publications, 7-9 Rathbone Street, London, W1P 1AF

Edited by Tony Hogg & Tony McDonald
Design & production: Footy Ltd & Independent UK Sports Publications
Print: Polar Print Group (Leicester)

The publishers would like to thank the following Hammers' fans for their help in producing this book. Alan Jacobs, for opening up his treasure trove of memorabilia; Stephen Marsh; Terry Connelly; Steve White of Footy Ltd; Danny Francis, photographers Steve Bacon (Newham Recorder), Malcolm Craig (Barking & Dagenham Post); John Bolle'; Richard Austin and the late Albert York.

Right: The Memorial Grounds main stand.
Facing page: Castle Street, circa 1905.

the early IRON AGE

THE WEST HAM UNITED STO[RY]

One of a series of picture story books publis[hed by] the London Evening Standard newspaper in November 1960.

THE 1890'S ··· A TIME OF GREAT SIGNIFICANCE IN TWO SECTIONS OF BRITISH LIFE ····

SOUTH WEST HAM, LONDON, ELECTED THE FIRST-EVER LABOUR M.P. AMID A THOUSAND CHEERS!

WHILE, TO A DWINDLING AUDIENCE, THE EAST END'S TWO MAIN FOOTBALL CLUBS PLAYED OUT THEIR LAST MATCHES ····

ON THIS BARREN SOCCER SCEN[E] A NEW CLUB, THAT WOULD GROW THROUGH THE DECADE[S] TO DWARF ITS PREDECESSOR[S] WAS ABOUT TO BE BORN ····

FOOTBALL IN LONDON'S EAST END WAS AT A LOW EBB WHEN, IN 1895, THE "THAMES IRONWORKS GAZETTE" MADE AN ANNOUNCEMENT ....

IT SAYS HERE, "MR. TAYLOR, WHO IS WORKING IN THE SHIPBUILDING DEPARTMENT, HAS UNDERTAKEN TO GET UP A FOOTBALL CLUB FOR NEXT WINTER ...."

THE THAMES IRONWORKS G

THE "HAMMERS" WERE ON THEIR WAY!

W·2

THAMES IRONWORKS PLAYED SOME OF THEIR EARLY GAMES IN 1895 BY FLOODLIGHT ....

THEIR SYSTEM WAS MORE AMBITIOUS THAN PERFECT!

THE LIGHTS WERE TOO LOW

COR ....WHERE DID THAT ONE GO?

AND EVERY FEW MINUTES THE GAME WAS STOPPED TO DIP THE BALL IN A BUCKET OF WHITEWASH!

W·3

May "West Ham" still remain "United."

Friends of the winter game,
  Patrons assembled here,
Most proud are we to name
  The favorites we hold dear;
Then let a "three times three"
  From this vast concourse rise,
And laud both loud and heartily
  The stalwart West Ham boys,
Whose claim to fame can not be slighted
  So long as they remain "United."

Will you that claim resist
  Ye men of Canning Town?
The song is seldom missed
  Until the bird has flown;
Will ye withhold support?
  'Tis all their leaders ask,
Your men have "held the fort,"
  Proved equal to the task,
Assist to make the outlook brighter,
  'Twill make Lew Bowen's heart feel lighter.

Go! travel if you will
  Great Britain round and round,
O'er valley, dale, and hill,
  Where battlefields abound,
You may find on your way
  Spots hallowed and renowned
But none to bear the palm away
  From your Memorial ground,
'Tis there in future years we ought
  To see the English Final fought.

Your favorites still maintain
  Their quenchless dash and go,
When did their courage wane
  Against their worthiest foe?
Then carol forth your song,
  The welcome theme renew,
Repeat the chorus loud and long,
  Cling to the old "Light Blue,"
Whate'er in future may betide them
  As staunch supporters stand beside them.

A.C., *Cricket Rhymester.*

Arnold Hills, the founder of Thames Ironworks.

The Boleyn Ground, circa 1905, looking towards the south-west corner, showing the old directors' pavilion and the original West Stand.

Anne Boleyn appears to be walking in the Boleyn Castle gardens, but the castle was built in 1544, eight years after her execution.

WEST HAM UNITED
FOOTBALL Co., Ltd.

Reg. Office and Ground:
CASTLE ST., GREEN ST., EAST HAM.

FIFTEENTH ANNUAL

Handbook, 1d.

Season 1914-15.

SEASON TICKETS now on Sale.
Price, 22/6 & 17/6.   Reserved Seats, 30/-.
2/6 Reduction to Shareholders.
Apply at the Office on the Ground, Castle Street,
Green Street, East Ham.

BOYD Gold Medal PIANOS
Direct from the Factory to the Public.   For Cash or on
Instalments.   Sent Home on First Monthly Payment.

BOYD, Limited,
320-322, Barking Road, EAST HAM,
NEAR TOWN HALL.
Write for Illustrated Catalogue FREE.

ADIUM - BRITISH EMPIRE EXHIBITION WEMBLEY

CAMPBELL·GRAY LTD LONDON W

THE F.A. CUP FINAL — BOLTON WANDERERS

NUTTALL   HOWARTH   ROWLEY   SEDDON   PYM   JENNINGS   FINNEY

THE F.A. CUP FINAL — WEST HAM FOOTBALL TEAM.

KING (SEC'Y)   W. HENDERSON   S. BISHOP   G. KAY   A.E. HUFTON   J. YOUNG   J. TRESADERN   C. PAYNTER (TRAINER)

BROWN   V. WATSON   W. MOORE   J. RUFFELL

FA Cup 1923

England international Jimmy Ruffell held the record for 505 league appearances when he finished playing for West Ham in 1936.

Fashion show, 1929.

1926-27

1923-24

Stan Earle, one of the few players to be capped at both amateur professional level for England.

Syd King, who managed from 1900 to 1932, the year of his tragic death.

Syd Puddefoot, whose record-breaking £5,000 move to Falkirk in 1921 caused a sensation.

D. SHEA.

Danny Shea broke the British transfer record when he moved to Blackburn Rovers for £2,000 in 1913.

George Kay, who captained Hammers in the 1923 FA Cup Final – the first ever to be played at Wembley.

In civvies at Villa Park, 1923.

Official Programme of the WEST HAM UNITED FOOTBALL Co L^TD

Boleyn Ground, Castle Street, Upton Park

Directors—W. F. WHITE (Chairman), L. JOHNSON (Vice-Chairman), J. W. Y. CEARNS, A. C. DAVIS, G. F. DAVIS, H. IGGULDEN, and J. E. PRATT
Secretary—E. S. KING   Assistant—A. N. SEARLES

No. 30   Match No. 29   Price 2d.

FEBRUARY 6th, 1926

WEST HAM UNITED RES.
v.
FULHAM RES.
LONDON COMBINATION.   KICK-OFF AT 3.15 P.M.

BOLENIUM
(Pronounced BO-LENNY-UM)

Super-Garments
Worn by the man who knows

Bib and Brace - - - from 6/11
Boiler Suits - - - " 10/11
Jackets - - - " 6/11
Warehouse Coats - " 10/6

Ask your Outfitter or write us direct;

W. A. SMITH & Co., Ltd.
Boleyn Castle, UPTON PARK, E.13

going

Official Programme of the
WEST HAM UNITED
FOOTBALL Cº Lᵀᴰ
BOLEYN GROUND, GREEN STREET, UPTON PARK

Directors—W. F. WHITE (Chairman), L. JOHNSON (Vice-Chairman), J. W. Y. CEARNS, W. J. CEARNS,
A. C. DAVIS, G. F. DAVIS and F. R. PRATT.
Secretary—E. S. KING   Assistant—A. N. SEARLES

No. 17   Match No. 18

NOVEMBER 12th, 1927   Price 1d.

WEST HAM UNITED
v.
CARDIFF CITY

FOOTBALL LEAGUE—Div. I.   KICK-OFF AT **2.45** P.M.

Next Home Match:
MILLWALL V. BARKING
Monday, Nov. 14th.   Kick-off 2.30 p.m.

V. WATSON   H. CONWAY   E. FENTON   L. GOULDEN   J. COCKCROFT   J. WOOD

A. WALKER   J. BARRETT   J. COLLINS   A. CHALKLEY   J. MORTON   J. RUFFELL

WEST HAM FOOTBALL CLUB

Jim Barrett

STEPHEN MARSH

LEONARD GOULDEN   WEST HAM

All the Best Alan 51.91
from Len. Goulden

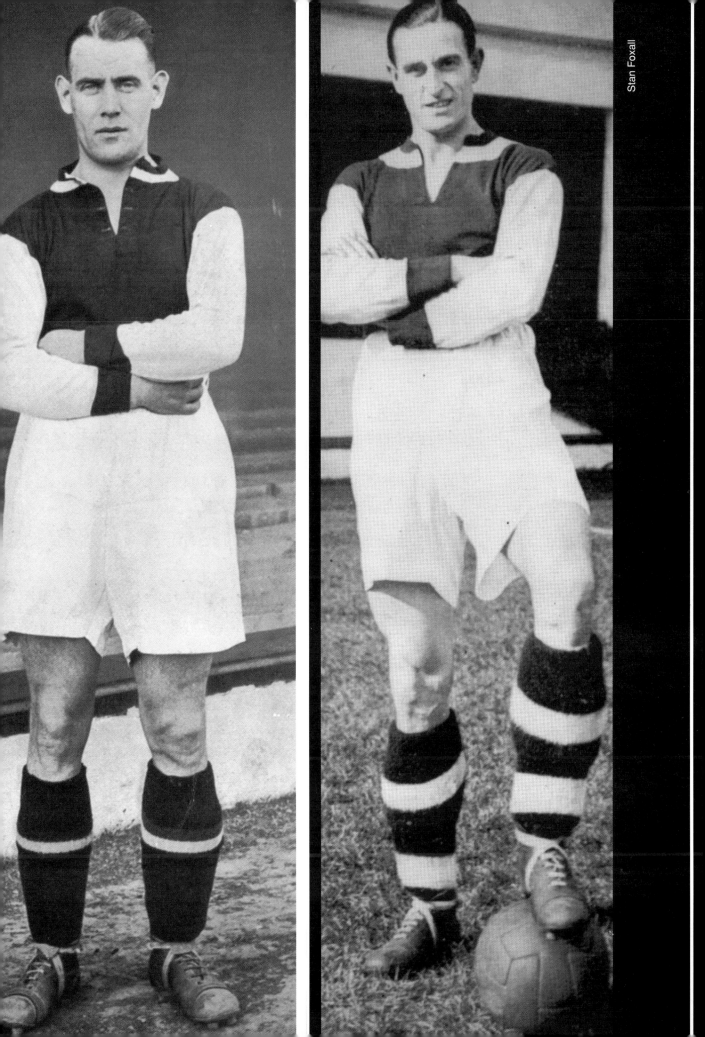

Stan Foxall

On April 29, 1937, an incredible crowd of 31,000 attended the London Combination League decider at Upton Park between West Ham Reserves and Arsenal Reserves. The team were locked together on 66 points going into the game . . . but Lewis scored for the Gunners to ensure the title went to Highbury.

Official Programme of the WEST HAM UNITED FOOTBALL Co LTD

BOLEYN GROUND. GREEN STREET. UPTON PARK

Directors :
W. J. CEARNS (Chairman), F. R. PRATT (Vice-Chairman), A. C. DAVIS, F. A. ENDERS, J. H. ROOFF, J.P.
Secretary : A. N. SEARLES

Price 1d.

APRIL 29th, 1937

No. 40

WEST HAM UNITED RES.
v.
ARSENAL Res.

KICK-OFF 6.30 P.M.

LONDON COMBINATION

FOOTBALL LEAGUE.—Div. II.

	P	W	D	L	For	Ag.	Pts.
	42	24	7	11	88	53	55
	41	23	8	10	85	56	54
Blackpool	42	22	5	15	74	56	52
Leicester City	41	22	8	12	80	52	49
Bury	42	22	8	12	71	55	47
Newcastle United	41	18	11	12	72	53	46
Plymouth Argyle	41	18	10	13	66	70	44
West Ham United	41	18	10	13	89	62	43
Sheffield United	41	16	12	14	87	59	43
Aston Villa	42	16	11	15	71	62	43
Tottenham Hotspur	41	17	9	13	64	54	40
Fulham	41	16	11	14	69	85	40
Coventry City	41	16	8	17	83	61	40
Blackburn Rovers	41	15	10	16	56	64	39
Chesterfield	41	15	9	17	49	70	36
Burnley	41	15	8	19	63	64	35
Barnsley	41	14	7	20	46	74	34
Norwich City	41	14	5	22	53	88	33
Swansea Town	41	13	11	12	18	52	30
Southampton	42	12	9	21	55	90	30
Bradford	41	12	9	20	65	94	30
Notts. Forest	41	11	12	21	54	83	24
Bradford City	42	9	7	10	24	30	24
Doncaster Rovers	41	7					

Next Home Matches:

FOOTBALL LEAGUE.—Div. II   3.30 p.m.

Sat., 1st May   SHEFFIELD UNITED

LONDON SENIOR CUP—FINAL   3.30 p.m.

Sat., 8th May   WALTHAMSTOW AV. v. HAYES

'PHONE ALBERT DOCK 1905

HELLIAR AND SONS, PRINTERS, 237 BARKING ROAD, PLAISTOW, E.13.

31,000

record attendance
v Arsenal reserves
Thursday April 29th, 1937

WEST HAM UNITED FOOTBALL CO. LTD

Registered Office - - BOLEYN GROUND
GREEN STREET, UPTON PARK, LONDON, E.13

Annual Official HANDBOOK

SEASON 1938-1939

PRICE
3d

E. FENTON (Half-back)
Born at West Ham
Previous Club: Fairbairn House
4 Seasons at West Ham
Height: 5ft. 11in. Weight: 11st. 6lb.

R. WALKER (Half-back)
Born at Hackney, London
Previous Club: Park Royal
5 Seasons at West Ham
Height: 6ft. Weight: 12st. 6lb.

J. COCKROFT (Half-back)
Born at Barnsley, Yorks
Previous Club: Gainsborough Trinity
5 Seasons at West Ham
Height: 5ft. 8in. Weight: 11st.

N. CORBETT (Half-back)
Born at Falkirk, Scotland
Previous Club: Heart of Midlothian
1 Season at West Ham
Height: 5ft. 11in. Weight: 11st. 10lb.

A. WEARE (Goalkeeper)
Born at Newport, Mon.
Previous Club: Wolverhampton Wanderers
2 Seasons at West Ham
Height: 6ft. Weight: 12st.

H. CONWAY (Goalkeeper)
Born at Gainsborough, Lincs.
Previous Club: Burnley
4 Seasons at West Ham
Height: 6ft. Weight: 12st. 2lb.

A. BANNER (Full-back)
Born at Sheffield, Yorks
Previous Club: Doncaster Rovers
3 Seasons at West Ham
Height: 6ft. Weight: 12st. 11lb.

C. WALKER (Full-back)
Born at Nottingham, Notts
Previous Club: Arsenal
2 Seasons at West Ham
Height: 5ft. 11in. Weight: 12st. 4lb.

H. MEDHURST (Goalkeeper)
Born at Byfleet, Surrey
Previous Club: Woking
3 Seasons at West Ham
Height: 5ft. 9in. Weight: 11st. 4lb.

C. BICKNELL (Full-back)
Born at Chesterfield, Derbyshire
Previous Club: Bradford City
5 Seasons at West Ham
Height: 5ft. 11in. Weight: 12st. 11lb.

A. CHALKLEY (Full-back)
Born at Plaistow, Essex
Previous Club:
7 Seasons at West Ham
Height: 5ft. 11in. Weight: 11st. 2lb.

S. FORDE (Full-back)
Born at Pontefract, Yorks.
Previous Club: Rotherham United
2 Seasons at West Ham
Height: 5ft. 11in. Weight: 11st. 6lb.

The year of 'The Fox'

Hammers' forward Sam Small is thwarted by Spurs 'keeper Percy Hooper in the second replay of the FA Cup fourth round tie at Highbury on February 2, 1939

In 1939 West Ham and Spurs were paired in the fourth round of the FA Cup at White Hart Lane. Winger Stan Foxall hit two goals to earn Irons a replay after they had been 2-0 down. After Archie Macaulay missed a penalty, Spurs went ahead again in the tie – only for Foxall to equalise and ensure a second replay at Highbury. In front of a 50,000 crowd, Hammers went behind for the third time in the tie, but 'The Fox' struck again when he latched on to a long clearance, held off the challenges of two defenders and scored with a low shot from outside the area. A crucial goal which led the way for Macaulay to atone for his earlier miss from the spot and hit the winner. True to nature, the Cockerels were killed off by 'The Fox'.

Arsenal Football Club Ltd.
Football   THE GUNNERS   League
First Division

PRICE 2d.

OFFICIAL PROGRAMME
SEASON 1938-39

1930s

WEST HAM UNITED F.C.

1937-38

John Young

Benny Fenton

Dick Walker

1938-39

1938-39

THE WAR
cup final

Captain Charlie Bicknell hoisted high by Herman Conway and Archie Macaulay.

Sam Small nets the winner.

EMPIRE  STADIUM

WEMBLEY

THE FOOTBALL LEAGUE

WAR

CUP FINAL

BLACKBURN ROVERS 0
v
WEST HAM UNITED 1

SATURDAY, JUNE 8TH, 1940

SIX

OFFICIAL PROGRAMME

The players are introduced to Field-Marshal Alexander prior to kick-off. The Hammers pictured are (left to right): Herman Conway, Charlie Bicknell, Len Goulden, Ted Fenton, Stan Foxall, George Foreman, Archie Macaulay, Joe Cockroft.

Action from the final.

up for the cup

Eddie and Ernie – the centurions

Eddie Chapman (holding the War Cup, which still remains in the Upton Park boardroom) was a loyal Hammer for 49 years as a player and club secretary. Ernie Gregory (with Sam Small, scorer of the winner) served the club for 51 years as goalkeeper and coach.

ain Charlie Bicknell receives the well-wishes from fans as Norman Corbett (in army fatigues) a swig from the cup. While, to his left, Ted Fenton, Archie Macaulay, George Foreman and Foxall lead the victory lap of honour around Wembley. Is that Eddie Chapman behind an?

quickest goal

eleven seconds

Saturday, 27th August, 1949 – Ken Bainbridge v. Barnsley

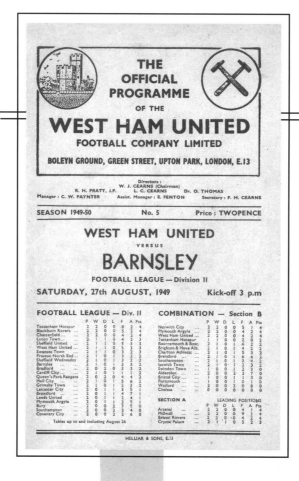

THE
OFFICIAL
PROGRAMME
OF THE
WEST HAM UNITED
FOOTBALL COMPANY LIMITED

BOLEYN GROUND, GREEN STREET, UPTON PARK, LONDON, E.13

Directors :
W. J. CEARNS (Chairman)
R. H. PRATT, J.P.   L. C. CEARNS   Dr. O. THOMAS
Manager : C. W. PAYNTER   Assist. Manager : E. FENTON   Secretary : F. H. CEARNS

SEASON 1949-50   No. 5   Price : TWOPENCE

WEST HAM UNITED
VERSUS
BARNSLEY
FOOTBALL LEAGUE — Division II
SATURDAY, 27th AUGUST, 1949   Kick-off 3 p.m.

FOOTBALL LEAGUE — Div. II

	P	W	D	L	F	A	Pts
Tottenham Hotspur	2	2	0	0	8	2	4
Blackburn Rovers	2	2	0	0	5	2	4
Chesterfield	2	2	0	0	4	2	4
Luton Town	2	1	1	0	4	2	3
Sheffield United	2	1	1	0	5	3	3
West Ham United	2	1	1	0	5	3	3
Swansea Town	2	1	1	0	3	2	3
Preston North End	2	1	0	1	3	2	2
Sheffield Wednesday	2	1	0	1	3	3	2
Barnsley	2	1	0	1	3	3	2
Bradford	2	0	2	0	3	3	2
Cardiff City	2	1	0	1	1	1	2
Queen's Park Rangers	2	0	2	0	4	4	2
Hull City	2	1	0	1	5	6	2
Grimsby Town	2	1	0	1	2	3	2
Leicester City	2	0	1	1	3	5	1
Brentford	2	0	1	1	4	7	1
Leeds United	2	0	1	1	2	4	1
Plymouth Argyle	2	0	1	1	1	4	1
Bury	2	0	0	2	3	5	0
Southampton	2	0	0	2	2	4	0
Coventry City	2	0	0	2	2	6	0

Tables up to and including August 26

COMBINATION — Section B

	P	W	D	L	F	A	Pts
Norwich City	2	2	0	0	5	1	4
Plymouth Argyle	2	2	0	0	4	2	4
West Ham United	2	2	0	0	4	2	4
Tottenham Hotspur	2	1	0	0	2	2	3
Bournemouth & Bosc.	2	1	0	1	6	2	2
Brighton & Hove Alb.	2	1	0	1	4	2	2
Charlton Athletic	2	1	0	1	5	3	2
Brentford	2	1	0	1	6	5	2
Southampton	2	1	0	1	4	4	2
Ipswich Town	2	1	0	1	2	3	2
Swindon Town	2	0	1	1	2	3	0
Aldershot	2	0	0	2	3	7	0
Bristol City	1	0	0	1	1	3	0
Portsmouth	1	0	0	1	0	1	0
Watford	2	0	0	2	0	8	0
Chelsea	0	0	0	0	0	0	0

SECTION A   LEADING POSITIONS

	P	W	D	L	F	A	Pts
Arsenal	2	2	0	0	4	1	4
Millwall	2	2	0	0	9	1	4
Bristol Rovers	2	2	0	0	4	2	4
Crystal Palace	2	1	1	0	5	2	3

HELLIAR & SONS, E.13

ELEVENTH HEAVEN...

Top right: Ken Bainbridge scored after only 11 seconds in the Second Division match against Barnsley.

Right: The second fastest Hammers scorer . . . Leroy Rosenior, who scored after only 17 seconds at Nottingham Forest on May 18, 1989.

Full-back Jack Yeomanson played for West Ham between 1947 and 1950 in 106 league and five FA Cup matches. His contract of employment is reproduced here.

An Agreement made the Thirteenth

day of May 1949 between Frank Horace Cearns of 21 Lancaster Road Forest Gate in the COUNTY OF London

the Secretary of and acting pursuant to Resolution and Authority for and on behalf of the West Ham United FOOTBALL Club of Upton Park London (hereinafter referred to as the Club)

of the one part and Jack Yeomanson of 120 Ramsgate Road Margate in the County of Kent Professional Football

(hereinafter referred to as the Player) of the other part **Whereas** agreed as follows :—

1. The Player hereby agrees to play in an efficient manner and to the best of his ability for the Club.

2. The Player shall attend the Club's ground or any other place decided upon by the Club for the purposes of or in connection with his training as a Player pursuant to the instructions of the Secretary, Manager, or Trainer of the Club, or of such other person, or persons, as the Club may appoint. [This provision shall not apply if the Player is engaged by the Club at a weekly wage of less than One Pound, or at a wage per match.]

3. The Player shall do everything necessary to get and keep himself in the best possible condition so as to render the most efficient service to the Club, and will carry out all the training and other instructions of the Club through its representative officials.

4. The Player shall observe and be subject to all the Rules, Regulations and Bye-Laws of The Football Association, and any other Association, League or Combination of which the Club shall be a member. And this Agreement shall be subject to any action which shall be taken by The Football Association under their Rules for the suspension or termination of the Football Season, and if such suspension or termination shall be decided upon the payment of wages shall likewise be suspended or terminated, as the case may be.

5. The Player shall not engage in any business or live in such place as the Directors (or Committee) of the Club may deem unsuitable.

9. In consideration of the observance by the said player of the terms, provisions and conditions of this Agreement, the said Frank Horace Cearns on behalf of the Club hereby agrees that the said Club shall pay to the said Player the sum of £11 : 0 : 0 per week from 1st August 1949 to 6th May 1950 and £10 : 0 : 0 per week from 7th May 1950 to 29th July 1950.

10. This Agreement (subject to the Rules of The Football Association) shall cease and determine on 29th July 1950 unless the same shall have been previously determined in accordance with the provisions hereinbefore set forth.

Fill in any other provisions required.

The said player to receive £1 : 0 : 0 per week extra when playing in First team.

As Witness the hands of the said parties the day and year first aforesaid

Signed by the said Jack Yeomanson and Frank Horace Cearns.

In the presence of

(Signature) Ben Guy

(Occupation) Clerk

(Address) 100, Fercles Rd Southend-on-Sea

J Yeoman— (Player).

F H Cearns. (Secretary).

Jack Yeomanson

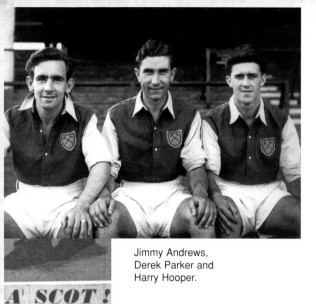

Jimmy Andrews,
Derek Parker and
Harry Hooper.

John Bond and Peter Chiswick.

John Dick

Derek Parker

soccer

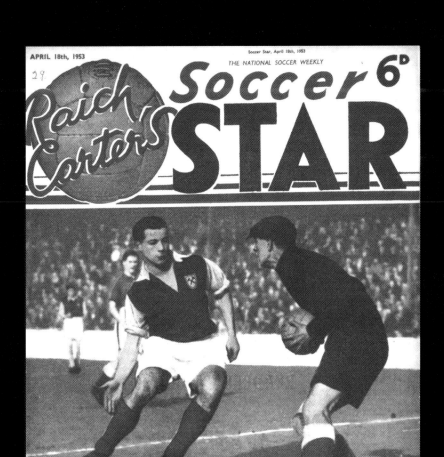

6ᴰ

stars ✦

UNDER THE LIGHTS

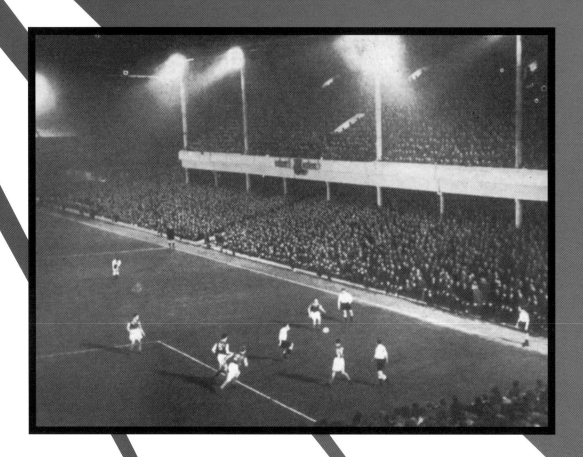

FITNESS IN THE FIFTIES

Top right:
Ted's team talk . . . (left to right): Malcolm Musgrove, George Wright, Derek Parker, Ernie Gregory, Terry Woodgate, Harry Kinsell, manager Ted Fenton, Albert Foan, Gerry Gazzard, Jimmy Andrews and Frank O'Farrell.

Middle right:
Eric Armstrong, Bill Nelson, Noel Cantwell, Jimmy Andrews and Dave Sexton.

Bottom right:
John Bond, Malcolm Allison, Mal Musgrove and Billy Dare.

Above:
Ron Cater, Albert Foan and Vic Niblett.

ft:
rst floodlight match at Upton
. . Thursday, April 16, 1953,
Ham 2, Spurs 1.

22, 1954, West Ham 3, St.
1. Peter Chiswick saves.

Champions! 1958

Howzat! Three former Hammers ready for cricket action with Essex Boys against Kent at Canterbury in 1957. Brian Edmeads, who later became a big star for the county, is pictured second from right in the front row.

Bobby Moore

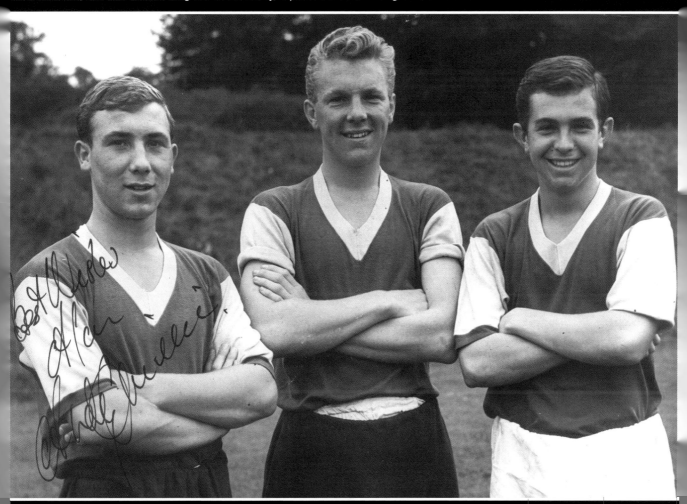

the
sixties

First Division champions Burnley v West Ham, Tuesday, April 11, 1960

September 26, 1964:
Johnny Byrne picks his spot
against Sheffield United.

January 21, 1961:
Mal Musgrove goes close
against Chelsea, with John
Dick in close attendance.

March 24, 1962:
Manchester City's famous
German 'keeper Bert
Trautmann saves from
Ron Tindall.

November 12, 1966:
Martin Peters guards the West Ham goal under the lights at White Hart Lane as Tottenham trio Dave Mackay, Alan Gilzean and Jimmy Greaves close in. Hammers won the thriller 4-3.

April 16, 1965 . . . a Good Friday for Brian Dear, seen scoring one of his historic five against West Brom in a 6-1 thrashing, much to the delight of the fans packed onto the old Souith Bank terrace.

April 9, 1966:
After winning 4-1 at Spurs the previous day, West Ham were on the receiving end at Chelsea to the tune of a 6-2 defeat. Jim Standen and Dave Bickles are helpless as Bobby Tambling scores, watched by grounded team mates Peter Osgood and George Graham.

February 12, 1966:
John Byron scores for Blackburn Rovers at the South Bank end past Jim Standen, with Eddie Bovington, Martin Peters and Ken Brown looking on. This FA Cup fourth round tie finished 3-3.

eft:
ember 20, 1965:
ny Byrne helps to clear up at
North Bank end, Highbury.

om left:
no! Arsenal score, watched by
jected Bobby Moore.

ch 27, 1965:
Sealey tussles with his
nal wing counterpart George
strong in Hammers' 2-1 victory
ton Park.

t:
ober 28, 1967:
1 win at Stamford Bridge, as
n Dear (hidden by post)
aims Geoff Hurst's goal while
sea's John Boyle, Ron Harris,
r Bonetti, Eddie Macreadie
Marvin Hinton despair.

FOR ENGLAND

Tony Cottee - pictured in his England under-21 days. He went on to win seven full caps, but did not complete the full 90 minutes once.

Johnny Byrne in action for England (centre) against Republic of Ireland and scoring against Uruguay at Wembley (above) in 1964. 'Budgie' won 10 caps as a Hammer.

39 steps to heaven . . . July 30, 1966, the day three West Ham legends conquered the world. Skipper Bobby Moore leads his England team mates, including hat-trick hero Geoff Hurst and the other scorer in the epic 4-2 triumph, Martin Peters, down the Wembley steps and into immortality.

WEST

Johnny Byrne watches Ronnie Boyce's shot beat David Gaskell – one of his two goals that helped Hammers to a memorable semi-final triumph over red-hot favourites Manchester United, who included all-time greats Bobby Charlton, George Best and Denis Law in their line-up. The match was played in torrential rain.

SHEFFIELD WEDNESDAY F.C. LTD.
HILLSBOROUGH, SHEFFIELD
FOOTBALL ASSOCIATION CHALLENGE CUP
SEMI-FINAL

LEPPINGS LANE

Saturday, 14th March
KICK-OFF 3 o'clock

ENTRANCE

B

GROUND 5/-

Issued subject to the Rules, Regulations and
Bye-Laws of the Football Association
No Ticket exchanged nor money refunded

Nº 05062

General Manager and Secretary
THIS PORTION TO BE RETAINED

YOU ARE REQUESTED TO TAKE
UP YOUR POSITION THIRTY
MINUTES BEFORE KICK-OFF

Bobby Moore and Jim Standen combine to foil the menace of Denis Law.

WEST HAM
1964
The Official Publication
of the West Ham Players
Price 2/6

FA Cup semi-final, Hillsborough, Sheffield
Saturday, March 14, 1964

West Ham United 3
Manchester United 1

Jim Standen makes a great save from David Herd.

The original F.A. Cup was stolen in 1895.

Aston Villa have won the Cup most times—seven.

The Cup competition was launched in 1871 on £1 13s. 5d.!

Newcastle have most Wembley Final appearances—ten.

FINAL FAC...

THE CUP

Wembley Day Of Soccer Glory

By VICTOR RAILTON

WEST HAM, the Cockney club from London's East End, measure their footballing strength against Preston North End, the pride of Lancashire, in what could be the match of the year at Wembley Stadium.

This FA Cup Final, the 36th at Wembley and the 83rd since the competition began, is more than just a South versus North meeting.

Preston were once expelled from the Cup tournament.

☆

Biggest Final win : 6—0 by Bury in 1903.

No Cup Final has been drawn since 1912.

☆

To-day's Cup Final is the 36th at Wembley.

FINAL

Manager Ron Greenwood took the team to West Ham greyhound stadium, Custom House, for training prior to the cup final – so that the players could practice on the the type of lush surface they would find at Wembley. Greenwood tests the turf with Johnny Byrne and Bobby Moore.

Captains meet: Bobby Moore and Preston's Nobby Lawton.

kick

FA Cup Final
Saturday, May 2, 1964
West Ham United 3
Preston North End 2

THE EMPIRE STADIUM · WEMBLEY

TABLE PLAN
AND
LIST OF THE GUESTS
at the
Luncheon
given by the
Chairman and Directors of
Wembley Stadium Limited
on the occasion of
THE FOOTBALL ASSOCIATION
CUP COMPETITION
FINAL TIE

PRESTON NORTH END
v
WEST HAM UNITED

on Saturday, May 2nd, 1964

Guests are kindly requested to take their
seats in the Stadium not later than 2.40 p.m.

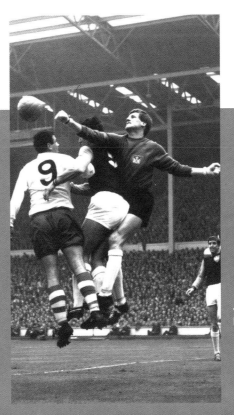

Jim Standen clears the danger as Alex Dawson puts the pressure on him and Ken Brown.

John Sissons puts Hammers ahead.

It might not have been the finest performance ever produced by West Ham, but goals by John Sissons, Geoff Hurst and a last-minute headed winner by Ronnie Boyce brought the FA Cup to Upton Park for the first time.

WEST HAM UNITED F.C.

H. SAMUEL

Well Done HAMMERS

ing For The Hammers

IE HOME!

charity
shield

August 15, 1964, Anfield
Liverpool 2
West Ham United 2

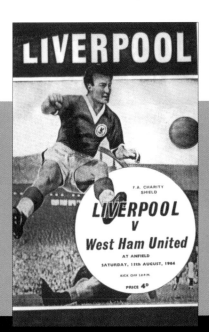

Right: Geoff Hurst scoops the ball past Tommy Lawrence.
Below: Honours even, as Bobby Moore and Ron Yeats share the shield.

It's there! Brian Dear opens the scoring in the 33rd minute of the quarter-final, first leg, against Lausanne.

Geoff Hurst fires in a shot against Lausanne of Switzerland in the quarter-final, second leg, at Upton Park, watched by Ken Brown and Johnny Byrne.

Sealey savages Lions

EUROPEAN CUP WINNERS' CUP

FINAL TIE
TSV MÜNCHEN 1860
v
WEST HAM UNITED

MAY 19th 1965 **WEMBLEY** Kick-off 7.30 p.m

OFFICIAL PROGRAMME . . . . ONE SHILLING

May 19, 1965, Wembley
West Ham United 2
TSV Münich 1860 0

The goals that won the cup. Right-winger Alan Sealey emerged as the hero of Wembley and the conqueror of the Lions of TSV Munich as West Ham became only the second English club to triumph in the European Cup Winners' Cup Final.

KINGS OF EUROPE!

The greatest night in Hammers' history . . . . proud conquerors of Europe after the 2-0 victory over TSV Münich 1860...

Facing page, top left:
Standing on the steps of Newham Town Hall, captain Bobby Moore and the Mayor, Alderman Terence C. McMillan.
Left: Munich 'keeper Radenkovic saves as John Sissons closes in.
Right: Martin Peters leads the victory lap of honour, while two-goal hero Alan Sealey and the skipper hold the cup aloft.
Bottom: Two-goal hero Alan Sealey.
This page:
Captain Fantastic, Bobby Moore, chaired by Martin Peters and Geoff Hurst. A year later, they went back to Wembley to conquer the World...

Night

Real FOOTBALL triumph with spec[...]

By BRIAN JAMES
West Ham 2 Munich 0

Cup of cups: Skipper Moore and scorer Sealey (left) troop the trophy.

WEST HAM last night gave Londoners the greatest football night of their lives and with it the European Cup Winners' Cup.

They beat Munich in a Wembley final of quite wondrous football to bring this trophy to London for the second time. Spurs won it two years ago in Holland.

The greatest

But more than the silver it will be the spectacle this crowd will ever cherish. Yes, even that longest of hours when West Ham brought Munich breathless to the brink of defeat then missed open goals.

The Germans, these skilled, powerful athletes, were not finally destroyed until the 68th and 70th minutes when West Ham's Cockney outside right, Alan Sealey, slammed two superb shots.

Wembley last night not only watched perhaps the greatest club match I have ever seen, it was part of it.

Nearly 100,000 people, the largest night Soccer crowd

The man with nothing to say

JON'S SPORTING TYPES

Sealey (No. 7) leaps [...]
after scoring his second [...]

f nights

wd see West Ham
le and Sealey . . .

IT was not only a European Cup for West Ham, but the best football match I have seen at Wembley since the stadium opened 42 years ago.

I was there as a boy, and so were West Ham.

They were beaten then, but I do not think any club would have defeated West Ham last night.

What must be emphasised at once is that this brilliant Final revealed another break-through for British football even more significant than Tottenham's two years ago.

Then the Spurs stood head and shoulders taller than any team in Britain.

Last night West Ham surged towards their highest peak with everyone knowing that Manchester United, Liverpool and Leeds already are good enough to pursue them hotly on the road to success.

FASCINATION

It seemed that all Wembley knew this last night, for this was a stadium full of genuine football knowledge and enthusiasm. There did not seem to be an unwanted VIP or ticket-sponger anywhere. It was what made the occasion so very different from Wembley on Cup Final day.

It was also a match to go to the film library with the great game between Real Madrid and Eintracht in the final of the European Cup at Hampden Park in 1960.

The fascination of the midfield build-up, the accuracy of the passing, the intellectuality of the tactics, the first-half tension as goals were missed and shots brilliantly saved, the slow ascendancy of Moore and his defenders over the fast, quick-passing Munich inside forwards . . . all these phases

TENNIS   ATHLETICS

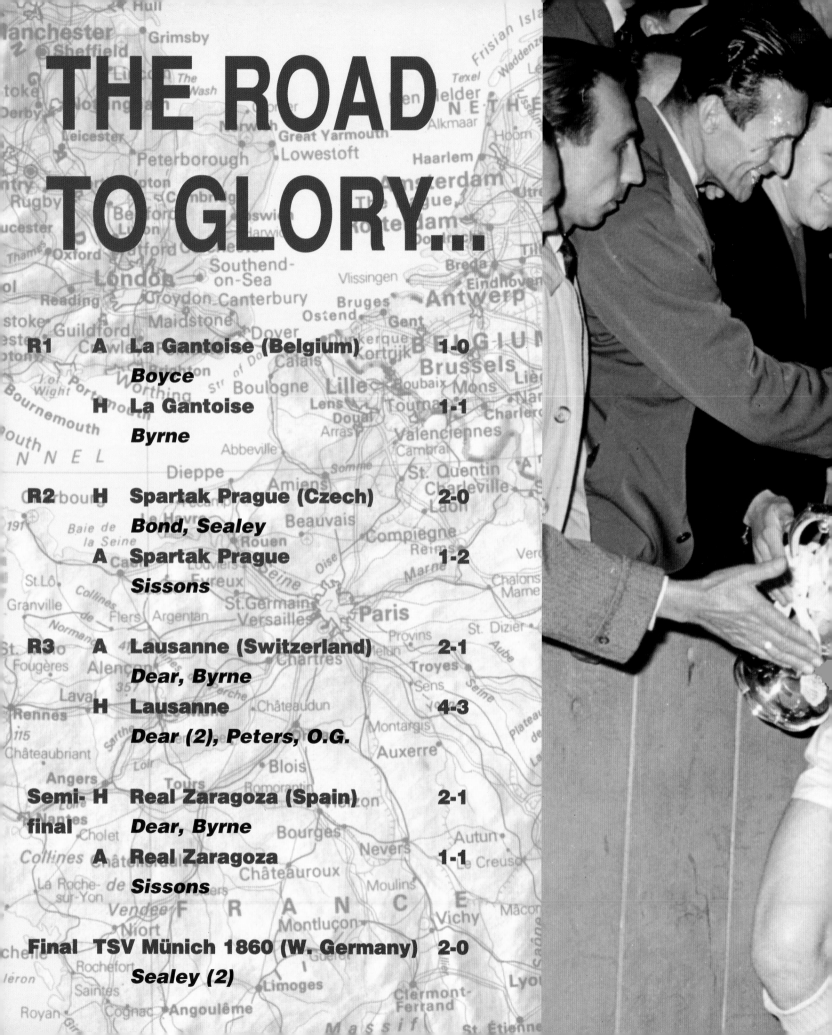

THE ROAD TO GLORY...

R1	A	La Gantoise (Belgium)	1-0
		Boyce	
	H	La Gantoise	1-1
		Byrne	
R2	H	Spartak Prague (Czech)	2-0
		Bond, Sealey	
	A	Spartak Prague	1-2
		Sissons	
R3	A	Lausanne (Switzerland)	2-1
		Dear, Byrne	
	H	Lausanne	4-3
		Dear (2), Peters, O.G.	
Semi-final	H	Real Zaragoza (Spain)	2-1
		Dear, Byrne	
	A	Real Zaragoza	1-1
		Sissons	
Final		TSV Münich 1860 (W. Germany)	2-0
		Sealey (2)	

In 1963, Josef Masopust, the famous Czechoslovak and Dukla Prague defender, predicted that West Ham would "win a European trophy within two years". He made his claim after Hammers had met Dukla Prague in the New York Soccer League in '63. How right he was!

Geoff Hurst leaps high above the Dukla Prague defence in the final of the American Challenge Cup at Randalls Island, New York, in the summer of 1963. West Ham lost the two-leg final, 2-1, but the experience of playing top class continental opposition laid the foundations for the European Cup Winners' Cup triumph in 1965.

Goalkeeper Jim Standen punches the ball clear in the semi-final against Gornik Zabrze of Poland, flanked by Jack Burkett (left) and skipper Bobby Moore.

Paul Brush

Trevor Brooking

Frank Lampard

Keith Colemen

Just three months into the 70s, Martin Peters (above) left for Tottenham in the deal that saw Jimmy Greaves switch to East London.

The much-travelled Bobby Gould (left), one of the game's true characters, was a crowd favourite in the mid-70s.

70s

Far left, top: March 1970, and Jimmy Greaves signs on for the fans on arrival at Upton Park.

Far left, bottom: January 12, 1974, and Billy Bonds scores in a 2-1 win over Manchester United. Clyde Best and Alan Wooler join in the celebrations as Martin Buchan looks on disconsolately.

Left: Striker Clyde Best, only the second black player (after John Charles) to play for Hammers.

Above: Geoff Hurst shows his strength in this challenge with Liverpool's Larry Lloyd.

Paying the penalty

Stoke win marathon tie

The League Cup, in all its many guises, has been a elusive trophy for West Ham. None more so than in season 1971/72 when after knocking out Cardiff C Leeds United, Liverpool and Sheffield United, Ham were drawn against Stoke City in the Semi-Final. T first leg was won 2-1 at the Victoria Ground with g from Geoff Hurst (penalty) and Clyde Best. But Ha lost the return leg 1-0 at Upton Park when the resu hinged on a dramatic last minute save by goalkeep Gordon Banks from his England team mate, Hurst' second penalty of the tie. The first replay was draw at Hillsborough, Sheffield, but the second replay a Trafford saw Hammers on the receiving end of a 5 thriller. Goals from Billy Bonds and Trevor Brookin could not prevent Hammers losing 3-2 in another h heavily influenced from the twelve yard spot, wher heroic stand-in goalkeeper Bobby Moore failed to Mike Bernard's twice struck penalty.

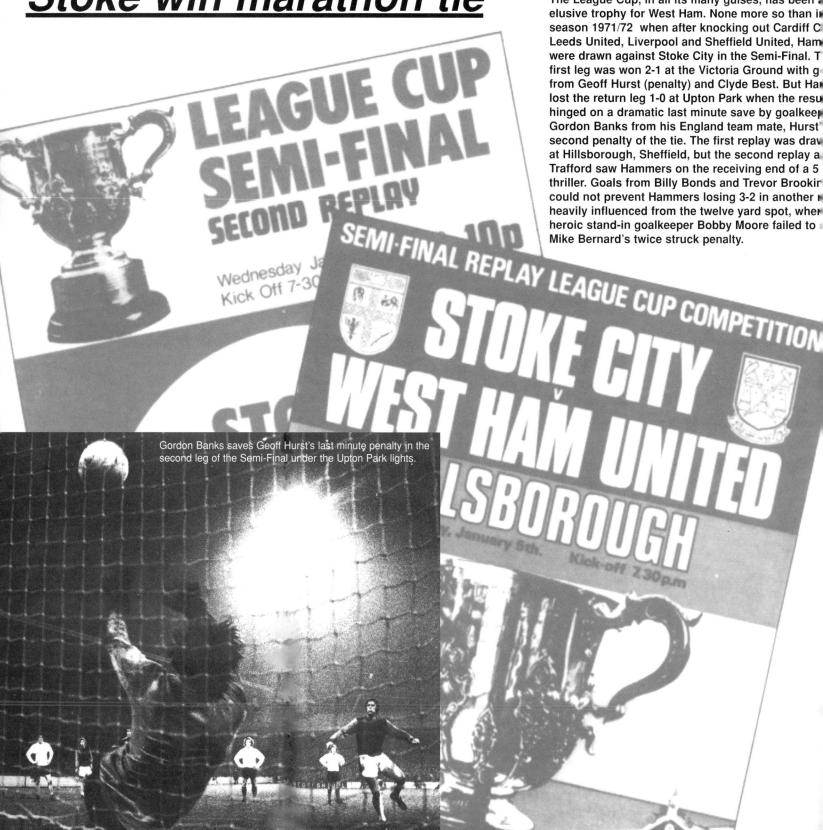

Gordon Banks saves Geoff Hurst's last minute penalty in the second leg of the Semi-Final under the Upton Park lights.

Bobby Moore dons injured Scottish International goal-keeper Bobby Ferguson's jersey. Then (above) saves Mike Bernard's first attempt, but just fails to beat out his follow-up shot.
(Right) The ball is firmly in the net and Stoke are on their way to Wembley, where they won their first major trophy in 109 years of trying by beating Chelsea 2-1.

Taylor-made

Alan's double spells Moore misery for Fulham

FA Cup Final
Saturday, May 3, 1975
West Ham United 2
Fulham 0

Alan Taylor, the £50,000 unknown winger from Rochdale, became West Ham's Wembley hero when he netted both goals in the victory over Second Division Fulham.

Above: Celebration time.
Above left: Billy Bonds and Graham Paddon console Bobby Moore, who had to settle for a losers' medal two years after leaving Upton Park for Craven Cottage.
Far left: Taylor shoots past the hapless Peter Mellor.
Middle left: Match-winner Taylor is congratulated by Billy Bonds and Trevor Brooking.
Left: Pat Holland and Billy Jennings parade the cup.

So near...
and yet so far

R1	A	Lahden Reipas (Finland)	2-2
		Brooking, Bonds	
	H	Lahden Reipas	3-0
		Robson, Holland, Jennings	
R2	A	Ararat Erevan (USSR)	1-1
		Taylor (A)	
	H	Ararat Erevan	3-1
		Paddon, Robson, Taylor (A)	
R3	A	FC Den Haag (Holland)	2-4
		Jennings (2)	
	H	FC Den Haag	3-1
		Taylor (A), Lampard, Bonds	
		(Agg 5-5; won on away goals)	
Semi-final	A	Eintracht Frankfurt (W.Ger.)	1-2
		Paddon	
	H	Eintracht Frankfurt	3-1
		Brooking (2), Robson	

| Final | Anderlecht (Belgium) | 2-4 |
| | *Holland, Robson* | |

Pat Holland (far right) scores West Ham's first goal, watched by team mate Billy Jennings (left).
Below: Frank Lampard tackles an Anderlecht forward while Pat Holland looks on anxiously.
Below left: Central defender Tommy Taylor trudges off as Billy Bonds examines his losers' medal.

Above: Billy Wright.
Top centre: Martin Hodge.
Top right: West Ham's scorer on Saturday Stuart Pearson.
Right: Billy Wright.
Far right: Phil Parkes.
Below: Trevor Brooking, Stuart Pearson (West Ham), Trevor Ross (Everton) at Villa Park on Saturday.

Football Association Challenge Cu

SEMI-FINAL REPLAY

WEST HAM UNITE
V EVERTON

ELLAND ROAD, LEEDS
WEDNESDAY 16th APRIL, 1980
Kick-off 7.45 p.m.

OFFICIAL SOUVENIR PROGRAMME 40

May 10, 1980, Wembley

West Ham United 1
Arsenal 0

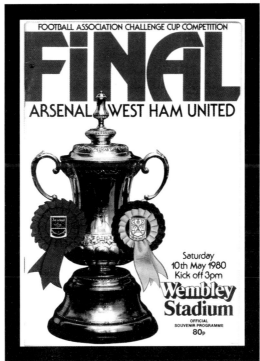

FOOTBALL ASSOCIATION CHALLENGE CUP COMPETITION

FINAL
ARSENAL v WEST HAM UNITED

Saturday
10th May 1980
Kick off 3pm

Wembley Stadium

OFFICIAL SOUVENIR PROGRAMME
80p

THE EMPIRE STADIUM, WEMBLEY
No ticket genuine unless it carries a Lion's Head watermark below

Football Association

F.A. CHARITY SHIELD

SAT., AUGUST 9, 1980

KICK-OFF 3.00 p.m.

YOU ARE ADVISED TO TAKE UP YOUR POSITION BY 2.30 p.m.

TURNSTILES D ENTRANCE 9

EAST UPPER STANDING ENCLOSURE

£2.50

STANDING

CHAIRMAN, WEMBLEY STADIUM LTD

SEE PLAN AND CONDITIONS ON BACK

TO BE RETAINED

THE EMPIRE STADIUM, WEMBLEY
No ticket genuine unless it carries a Lion's Head watermark below

The Football Association
Challenge Cup Competition

FINAL TIE

SAT., MAY 10, 1980

KICK-OFF 3.00 p.m.

YOU ARE ADVISED TO TAKE UP YOUR POSITION BY 2.30 p.m.

1. This ticket is not transferable.
2. This counterfoil must be retained for at least 6 months.

TURNSTILES H ENTRANCE 36 ROW 3 SEAT 20

CHAIRMAN, WEMBLEY STADIUM LTD

SEE PLAN AND CONDITIONS ON BACK

SOUTH STAND SEAT £16.00

TO BE RETAINED

cup final 1980. west ham versus arsenal

BILLY BONDS THE HAMMERS TOGETHER

CELEBI

F.A. CUP FINAL 1980

ARSENAL'S 3rd CONSECUTIVE FINAL

ARSENAL

versus

WEST HAM UNITED

OFFICIAL FOOTBALL LEAGUE
SERIES
SPECIAL EVENTS
SEASON 1979-80
NUMBER 10

WEST HAM UNITED FOOTBALL CLUB
Executive Club

Special
Cup Final Night

Dinner

Cabaret & Dance

★

THE SAVOY HOTEL
London, W.C.2

★

Saturday, 10th May, 1980
8.80 p.m. to 2.00 a.m.

ATIONS

Reception

to honour

West Ham United
Football Club

Football Association
Challenge Cup
Winners
Wembley 1980

Newham Town Hall

Wednesday, 16th July, 1980

London
Borough of Newham

THE F.A. CUP FINAL
10 MAY 80 WEMBLEY

10½P Buckingham Palace

MATCH RESULT

ARSENAL................0   WEST HAM UTD.............1

(Brooking)

class of '81

West Ham's famed 'Academy' produced many talented players who went on to become household names. The club reached the FA Youth Cup five times, two of which resulted in victories – in 1963 and 1981. This is the jubilant class of '81 after clinching a 2-1 aggregate victory over Tottenham at White Hart Lane. The team that night was: Vaughan, Keith, E. La Ronde, Dickens, G. Ampofo, McPherson, Barnes, Allen, Milton, Burvill, Schiavi.

Ray of hope

Above: David Cross makes for the dressing room at the end of a dramatic afternoon.

Below: Ray Stewart was West Ham's undisputed penalty king. The Scottish full-back scored 76 spot-kicks – missing only 10 – and this was the most important, his dramatic injury-time equaliser against Liverpool that earned Hammers a deserved replay at Villa Park. Alas, the Reds won that 2-1.

TREVOR BROOKING

Testimonial
Match
**WEST HAM
UNITED**
VERSUS
AN ENGLAND XI

Monday
31 October
1977

Boleyn Ground
London E.13

OFFICIAL PROGRAMME
FIFTEEN PENCE

trevor brooking

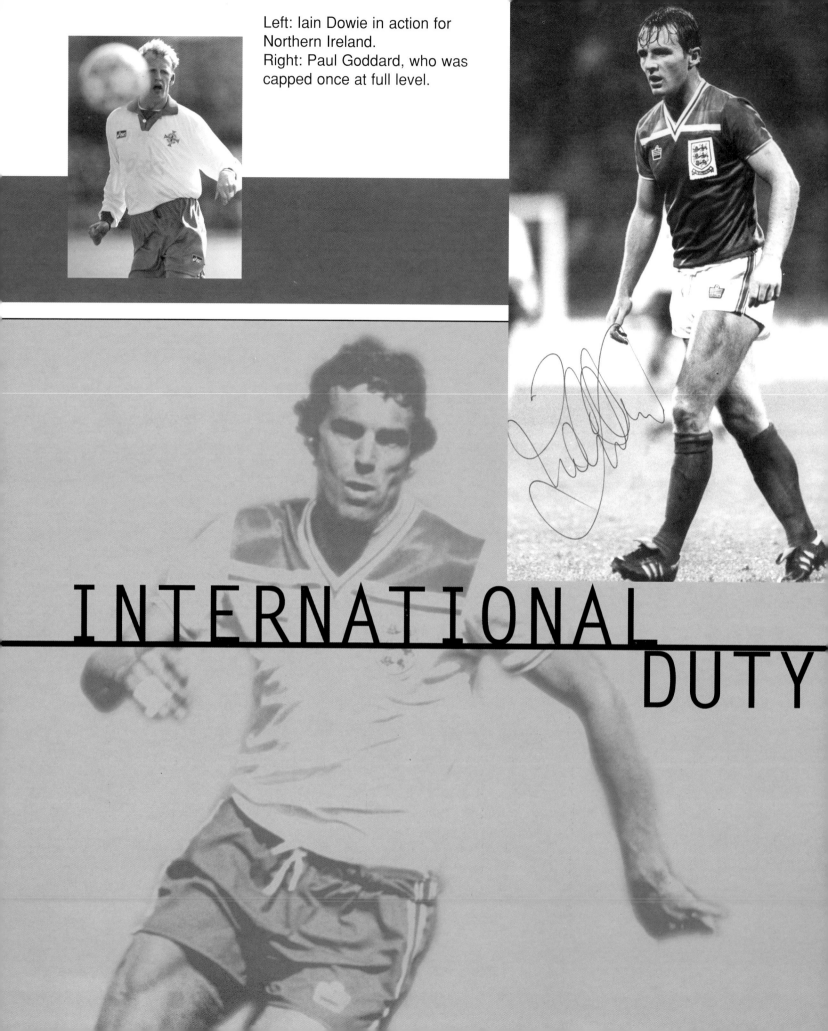

Left: Iain Dowie in action for Northern Ireland.
Right: Paul Goddard, who was capped once at full level.

INTERNATIONAL DUTY

Top left:
Alan Devonshire.
Left: Marc Rieper
flies the Danish
flag.
Right: Trevor
Brooking, one of
England's finest.

Frank McAvennie – one of the most popular and charismatic players ever to wear the claret and blue. In season 1985-86, the Scottish striker scored a sensational 26 league and two cup goals as Hammers challenged strongly for the old First Division championship (eventually finishing third) and reached the FA Cup quarter-finals. 'Macca's' strike partnership with Tony Cottee (who contributed a no less impressive 20 league and six cup goals) yielded 54 goals in total. West Ham has never enjoyed a more successful league campaign in its history than that exhilarating campaign.

	P	W	D	L	F	A	Pts
Liverpool	42	26	10	6	89	37	88
Everton	42	26	8	8	87	41	86
West Ham	42	26	6	10	74	40	84
Man Utd	42	22	10	10	70	36	76
Sheff Wed	42	21	10	11	63	54	73
Chelsea	42	20	11	11	57	56	71
Arsenal	42	20	9	13	49	47	69
Nottm F	42	19	11	12	69	53	68
Luton	42	18	12	12	61	44	66
Tottenham	42	19	8	15	74	52	65
Newcastle	42	17	12	13	67	72	63
Watford	42	16	11	15	69	62	59
QPR	42	15	7	20	53	64	52
Soton	42	12	10	20	51	62	46
Manchester	42	11	12	19	43	57	45
Aston Villa	42	10	14	18	51	67	44
Coventry	42	11	10	21	48	71	43
Oxford	42	10	12	20	62	80	42
Leicester	42	10	12	20	54	76	42
Ipswich	42	11	8	23	32	55	41
Birmingham	42	8	5	29	30	73	29
West Brom	42	4	12	26	35	89	24

FRANK

McAVENNIE

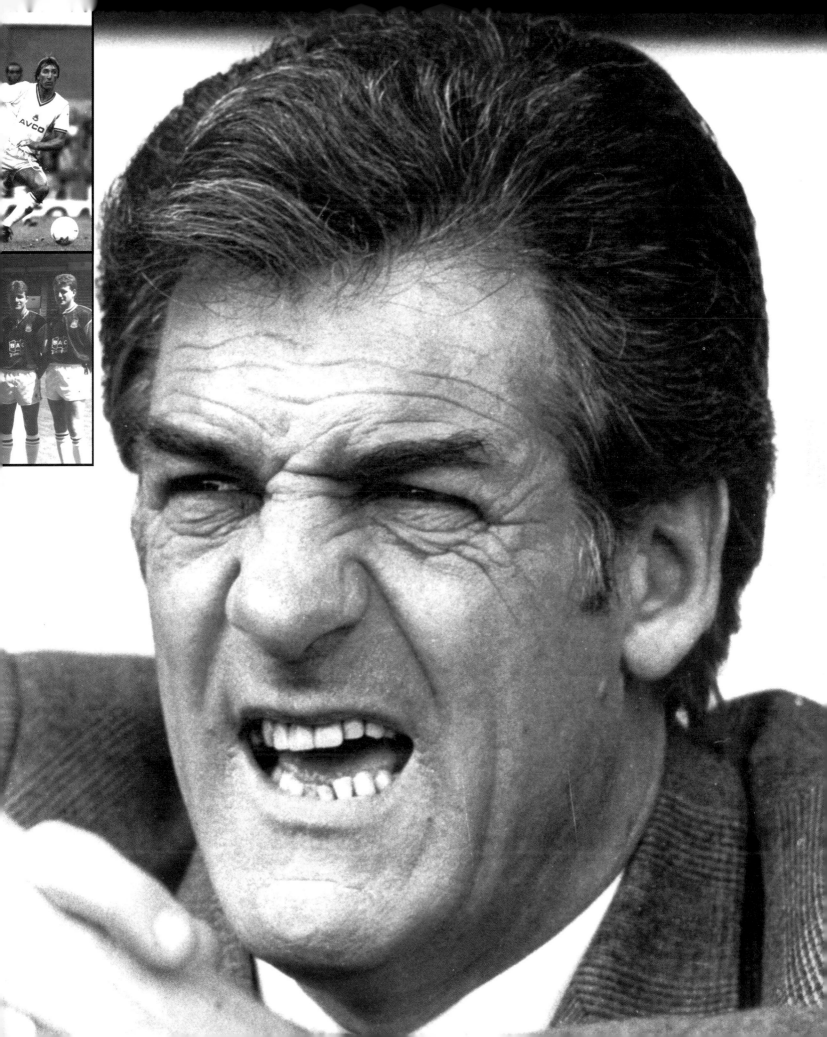

BILLY BONDS

julian dicks

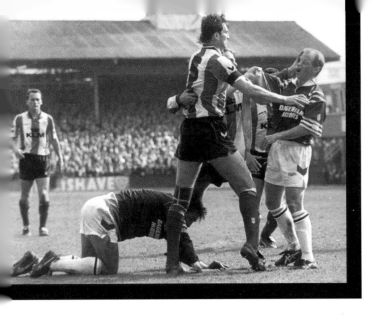

Left: David Speedie in typically confrontational pose during a match again[...] Brentford, 1993.

Above: Tim Breacker receiving congratulations.

Below: After the Dagenham Motors sponsorship deal was signed in 1992 Manager Billy Bonds is at the wheel, surrounded by Alvin Martin, Clive A[...] Julian Dicks, Tony Gale, Steve Potts and Stuart Slater.

Above: Tempers flair in a derby clash at the old Den, where Tim Breacker, George Parris and Alvin Martin get to grips with Millwall's Alex Rae.
Right: Clive Allen signals another goal in the 1992/93 promotion campaign, watched by Kevin Keen.

Above: Julian Dicks thumps home another penalty in the 1992/93 promotion season.
Right: Celebration time in the home dressing room after clinching promotion in the final game against Cambridge United, May 1993.
Below, left to right: Trevor Morley gets it in the neck from Arsenal's David Seaman. David Burrows and physio John Green have a count up. Billy Bonds and Harry Redknapp, former team mates and a new management partnership in August 1992. Tony Gale, who was awarded a testimonial in May 1994, given a free transfer and then won a Premiership winners' medal with Blackburn Rovers the following season. Stylish Ian Bishop on the ball. Tim Breacker, Bonzo's first signing in October 1990.

L U D O

RECORD BREAKER

Czechoslovakian International goalkeeper Ludek Miklosko had played in 176 consecutive League games up to 4th Nov 1996, including every Premiership fixture to that date. A record for a Hammers' goalie.

L
U
D
O

'He epitomised everything a great footballer should be. He was a master on the pitch and an ambassador for the game off it'
– *Ron Greenwood*

MO

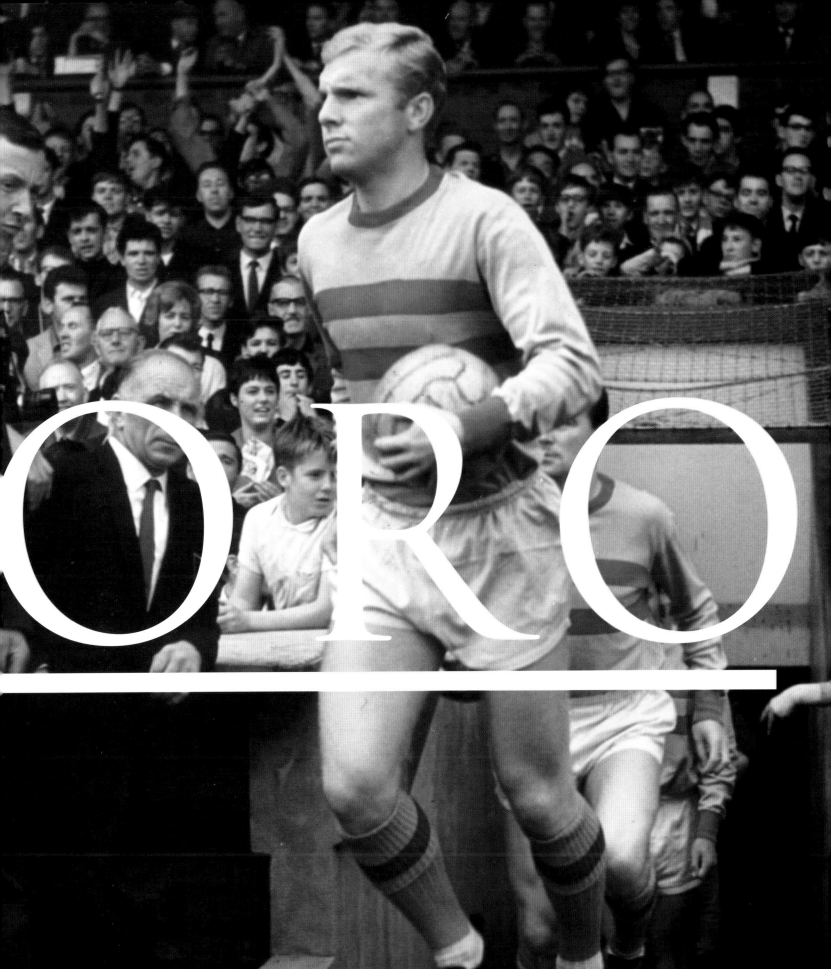

'In all the millions of sentences expended across endless miles of newsprint – as well as spoken on television and radio – there was not one critical word'
Jeff Powell, The Life and Times of a Sporting Hero

Below:
West Ham chairman Terry Brown and Bobby Moore's wife, Stephanie, seal the time capsule, carrying mementoes of Bobby's career, which is buried within the South Stand that was named after him.

It was early on the morning of February 24, 1993, that Bobby Moore passed away at his London home, almost two years after his cancer was diagnosed. His full importance to West Ham United, his enormous influence on and off the field, could not possibly be crammed into the pages of this book but the pictures tell their own story of a footballing legend who was loved and respected all over the world, not simply in the East End. Within minutes of hearing of his death, devastated supporters gathered outside West Ham's ground to mourn the loss of their all-time favourite. The big iron gates at the main entrance became a shrine to the legendary number six who will never be forgotten.

MOORE STAND

HAMMER

A TRIBUTE TO
A LEGEND
BOBBY MOORE, OBE.

BOBBY MOORE
Memorial Match
7th March
1994

v.

F.A. PREMIER LEAGUE X

The Bobby Moore bust that stands in the reception are of the South Stand named after West Ham's favourite son.

Hammers News, March 1994.

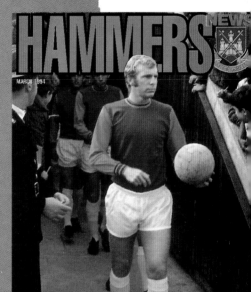

...nited: All of Mooro's team mates from ...1964 FA Cup and 1965 ECWC-winning ...ns came together again to pay tribute to ...maestro on the night of his memorial ...ch, between West Ham and a ...miership XI, at Upton Park, March 7, ...4. Johnny Byrne and John Sissons flew ...om South Africa, while Jim Standen ...e from USA to attend an emotional ...asion.

...cing page: The matchday programme ... the home game against Wolves – ...e first since Bobby's death – carried a ...ecial 16-page tribute to West Ham's ...est.

...set: The specially commissioned crest ...t was worn on the memorial match ...irts, which have become a collector's ...m.

Mrs Stephanie Moore meets the Hammers prior to Bobby's memorial match.

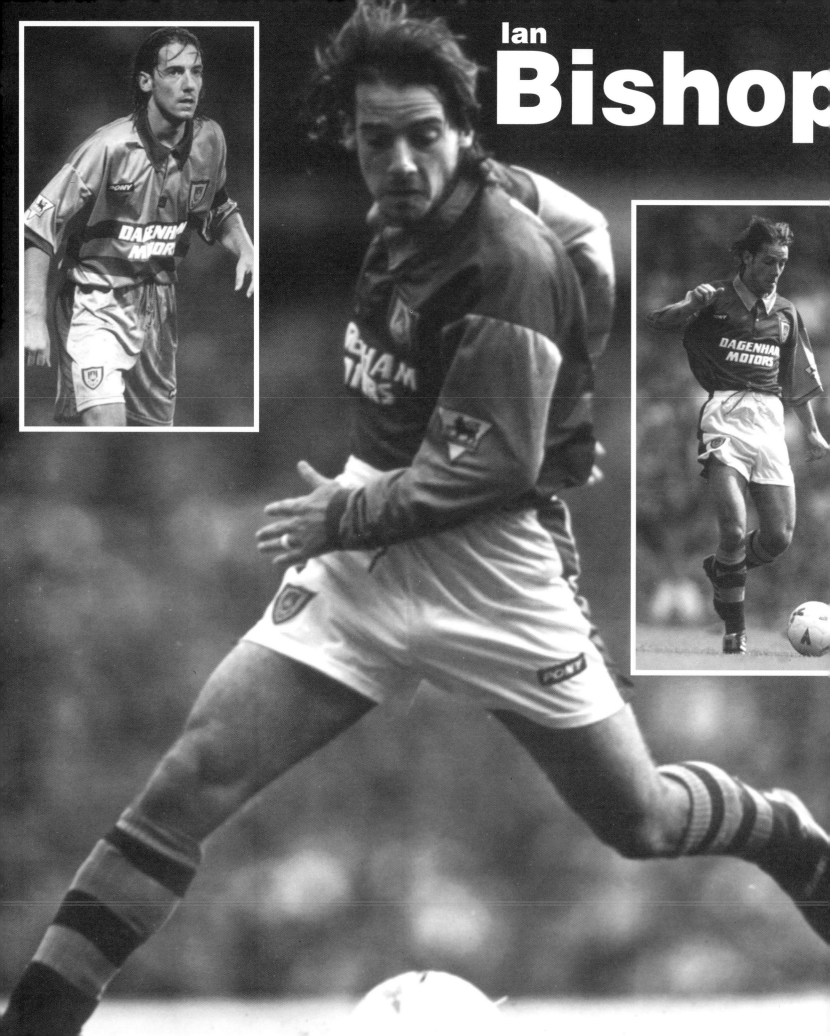

Ian Bishop

Steve
Potts

TONY COTTEE

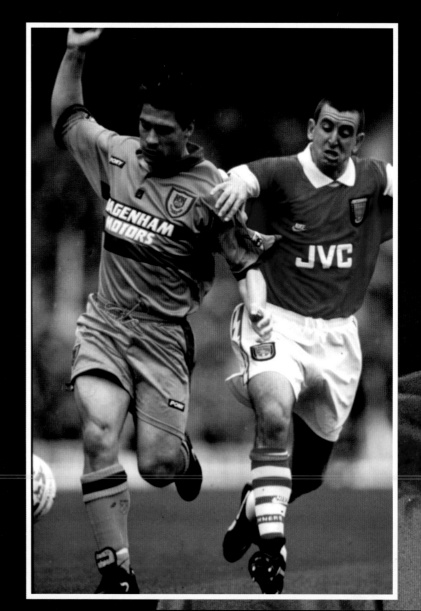

Established as the fifth highest goalscorer in Hammers' history, the prolific 'TC' never looked back after sensationally scoring on his debut against Spurs, aged 17, on New Year's Day, 1983. He became Britain's most costliest player when, in 1988, he joined Everton for £2.05 million. But after six turbulent years on Merseyside, he returned for a second spell at Upton Park.

ALVIN MARTIN became only the second Hammer since Billy Bonds to be awarded two testimonials by the club. The central defender from Liverpool arrived at Upton Park as a raw 16 year-old, made his first team debut in 1978 and rose to fifth in West Ham's all-time appearances list during the 1995/96 season – his last as a player – at the age of 37.

THE **ALVIN MARTIN**

TESTIMONIAL MATCH

WEST HAM UNITED

TOTTEN HOTS

SUNDAY 21st AUGUST 1988

KICK-OFF 3.00 p.m.

SOUV PROG

AVCO

ALVIN

Left: Holding the Second Division championship trophy in 1981.

Below: Still running the show at 37, 'Stretch' organising at the back as Julian Dicks turns for advice.

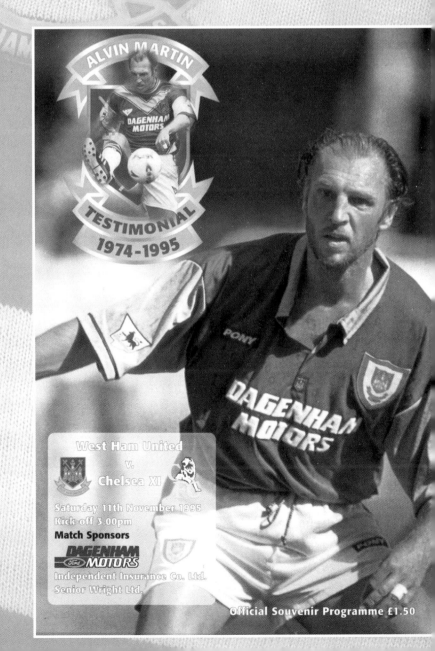

ALVIN MARTIN

TESTIMONIAL

1974-1995

West Ham United
v.
Chelsea XI

Saturday 11th November 1995
Kick-off 3.00pm

Match Sponsors

DAGENHAM *Ford* MOTORS

Independent Insurance Co. Ltd.
Senior Wright Ltd.

Official Souvenir Programme £1.50

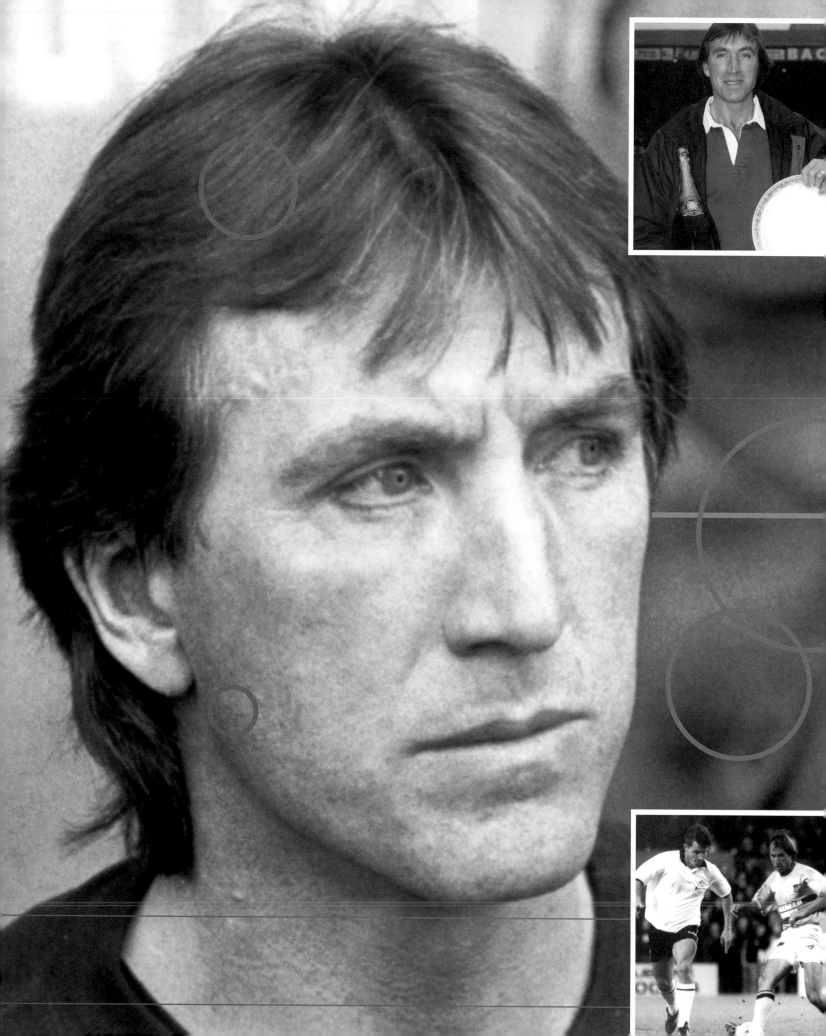

of the club's all-
 greats, Billy
ds made a record-
king 663 league
130 cup appear-
s from 1967 until
etired, aged 41, in
B. The battling
zo led Hammers to
FA Cup Final victo-
and was the first
mmer to be award-
wo testimonials in
-year playing
er. He was
pinted manager in
0 and twice got the
 promoted to the
light before he
gned in August
4.

BILLY BONDS
Testimonial Match
Monday 4 December 1978

WEST HAM
UNITED
versus
TOTTENHAM
HOTSPUR

BOLEYN GROUND
UPTON PARK
LONDON E.13

Official
Programme 15p

billy bonds

You're fan-tastic! Through the highs and the lows, West Ham has always enjoyed great loyal support.

I'm Forever

Tony Cottee (top) and
Kenny Brown (middle)
make time for their young
fans, while (bottom)
wingers Mark Robson and
Kevin Keen salute the fans
from the directors' box after
clinching promotion in May
1993.

blowing
bubbles

Eastenders

Football clubs are made up of all sorts of personalities – not all of them players or members of the management. On this spread, we look at some of the colourful characters who have been part and parcel of the Upton Park scene through the years...

FACING PAGE:
From the top:

Noel Cantwell with the Irishman, Paddy O'Leary, who went with him from Ireland to West Ham. Paddy used to lead out the team before home games in the 50s and 60s.

Stan Botham, former clerk of works and head groundsman, gets to grips with a snow-covered pitch.

Actors Leslie Grantham, Nick Berry and Michael Cashman were original stars of the BBC TV soap series Eastenders and regular visitors to Upton Park.

Official club photographer Steve Bacon and another Hammers celebrity fan, boxer Lennox Lewis.

Top right: Wally St. Pier, the former chief scout whose string of brilliant finds included the famous World Cup-winning trio.

Main picture:
An Alf Garnett lookalike. Garnett, played by actor Warren Mitchell (a Spurs fan in real life!), was the star of the long-running BBC TV series 'Till Death Us Do Part'.

COCKNEY PRIDE

In an increasingly cosmopolitan West Ham team of the 1990s, John Moncur, from Bethnal Green, represents one of the few genuine 'local lads' in the squad today.

JOHN MONCUR

IAIN DOWIE (Northern Ireland)

MARC RIEPER (Denmark)

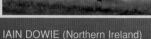

ROBBIE SLATER (Australia)

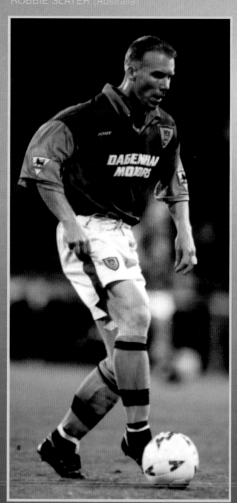

MICHAEL HUGHES
(Northern Ireland)

Legion

STAN LAZARIDIS (Australia)

MARCO BOOGERS (Holland)

LUDEK MIKLOSKO (Czech Republic)

KEITH ROWLAND (Northern Ireland)

The Management

Harry Redknapp and Frank Lampard

Harry Redknapp – a youngster in the squad of 1964/65.

Frank Lampard in the 1965 youth team (with Trevor Brooking next him) listening to manager Ron Greenwood.

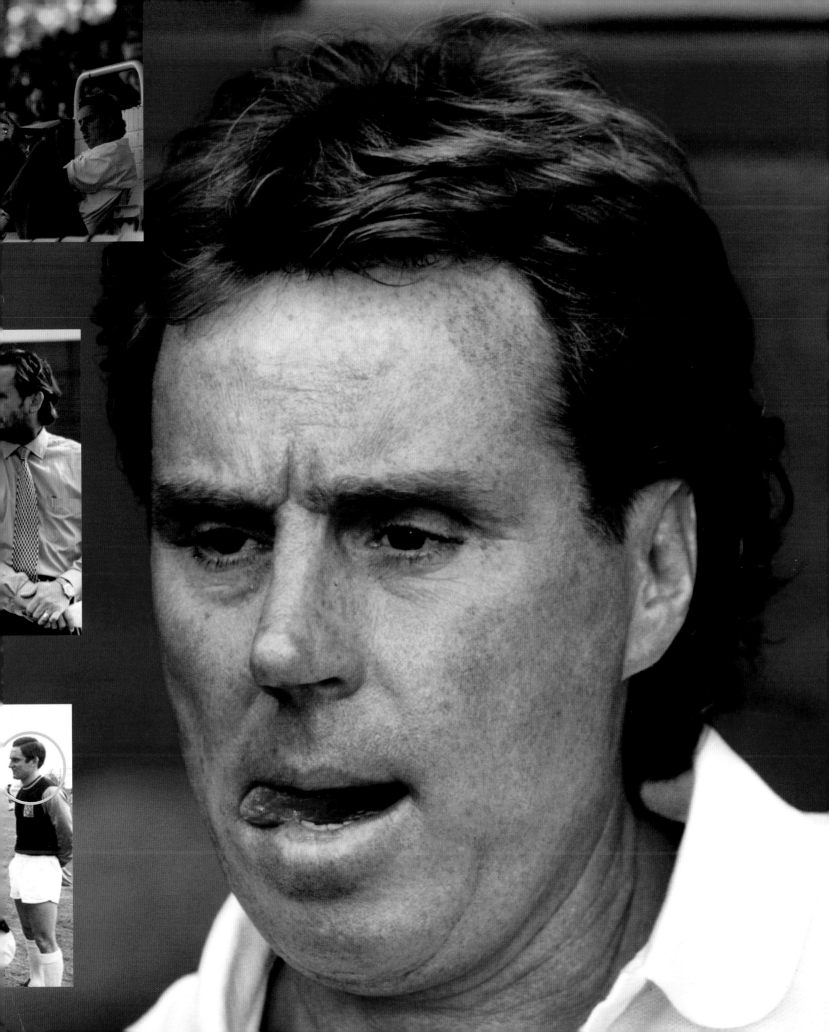

WEST HAM UNITED

WEST HAM UNITED

BOLEYN GROUND : LONDON
A.R.A LA GANTOISE (Belgium)
EUROPEAN CUP WINNERS CUP
Preliminary Round : Second Leg
WEDNESDAY 7th OCTOBER 1964 at 7.30 p.m.

WEST

BOLEYN G

OFFICIAL PROGRA

Directors: R. H

SEASON 19

WEST HAM FOOTBA

SATURDAY 8th MARCH 1958

Our

Club Notes

WEST HAM UNITED

LIVERPOOL
FOOTBALL LEAGUE—Division One
MONDAY 3rd SEPTEMBER 1962 at 7.30 p.m.

OFFICIAL PROGRAMME

WEST HAM UNITED

VERSUS
SUNDERLAND

FOOTBALL LEAGUE : Division One
Saturday 19th October 1968
KICK-OFF 3 p.m.

OFFICIAL PROGRAMME   No. 18   1/-

PROGR

A

FOO

M

HAMMER

AVCO TRUST OFFICIAL CLUB SPONSOR

BURY
Milk Cup Second Round
Second Leg

Tuesday 25 October 1983
Official Programme

Kick-Off 7.30 p.m.
50p

TONIGHT'S MATCH SPONSORED BY
UNIGATE DAIRIES
Unigate

HAMMER

AVCO TRUST OFFICIAL CLUB SPONSORS

The TODAY League Division One
ASTON VILLA
Saturday 22nd November 1986
Kick-off 3.00 p.m.
Official Matchday Programme

Hammer

Official Matchday Magazine

80p

The Barclays League Division One
NORWICH CITY
Saturday 29th August 1987
Kick-Off 3.00 p.m.

AVCO TRUST   OFFICIAL CLUB SPONSORS

TODAY'S MATCH
SPONSORED BY
SCORELINE

H

AMMES

The Club has always enjoyed a reputation for producing a matchday programme of the highest quality. Jack Helliar (inset) was responsible for printing and editing 'Hammer' for many years and since the early 80s, only three editors – Colin Benson, Tony McDonald and now Peter Stewart – have succeeded the late Press Officer, whose son, John, now manages the Press Room at Upton Park.

Last orders ...

WEST HAM

A to Z

1895-1995

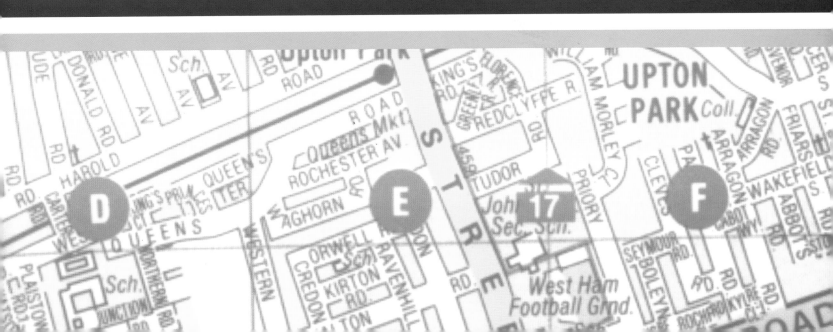

The Allen cousins:
Paul (top),
Clive (right)
and Martin (bottom).

A is for **Allen**, of whom three members of the same family played for Hammers. The first was Paul, who became the youngest player to appear in an FA Cup Final when he faced Arsenal in 1980, aged 17 years and 256 days. A year later, little 'Ollie' broke Bobby Moore's long-standing record of 18 England youth caps. Paul's cousin, Martin, helped Hammers to promotion in 1990/91 and was joined in the side by another cousin, Clive, for the successful 1992/93 First Division promotion campaign.

All-seater, the phrase adopted in Lord Justice Taylor's controversial report on ground safety in the wake of the 1989 Hillsborough Disaster. The main focus of his detailed report decreed that all Premier and First Divisions clubs had to convert their terraces to seats, which West Ham finally achieved with the opening of the two-tier Centenary Stand in January 1995.

Allison, the football visionary of the 50s who, under manager Ted Fenton, did more than anyone to establish West Ham United's famed youth 'Academy'. He held regular team meetings around the dinner table at Cassettari's Cafe in the Barking Road, just around the corner from the Boleyn Ground, where Malcolm and his 'disciples', Noel Cantwell John Bond, Dave Sexton, Jimmy Andrews, Frank O'Farrell and Mal Musgrove, talked tactics. Strongly influenced by the magnificent Magyars who outplayed England at Wembley in 1953, it was 'Big Mal' – forced to quit playing due to tuberculosis in 1958 – who introduced continental-style silky strip and lightweight boots.

All-ticket match, the first of which at Upton Park – since pre-war – was for the visit of Manchester United on May 16, 1977.

Ann Boleyn, who was rumoured to have stayed at Boleyn Castle. But the 'castle' was really a building known officially as Green Street House and was built in 1544 – eight years after the execution of Ann Boleyn

Appearance record, held by former captain Billy Bonds, who retired as a player in 1988, aged 41, after playing 663 league and 130 cup games for the club in a remarkable 21-year playing career. It is a proud record that will almost certainly never be emulated. Joe Cockroft holds the club record for successive appearances – 208, between 1932 and 1938. The wing-half played 263 games in all.

Astroturf. Hammers were

involved in the first professional matches to be played on astroturf and tartan turf. The matches were played in America, against Kilmarnock (astroturf) and Dundee United (tartan turf) in May 1969. Our first Football League match on plastic was played at Queens Park Rangers on February 7, 1984, a 1-1 draw in which Tony Cottee scored for Hammers.

Attendance record. The biggest official crowd recorded at Upton Park was 42,322 for the First Division match against Tottenham on October 17, 1970.

Avco Trust, the first official club sponsors of West Ham, whose six-year association began in 1983.

is for *BAC Windows*, who succeeded Avco as main sponsors in the summer of 1989 and continued until 1992.

Best-ever position in the top flight of English league football was achieved by John Lyall's team of 1985/86, which finished a very creditable third – behind Merseyside giants Liverpool and Everton. Hammers still had hopes of winning the title for the first time in their history right up until the final Saturday of the season but, despite a 3-2 victory at West Bromwich, it was Kenny Dalglish's winner for Liverpool at Chelsea that day which settled the thrilling title race issue. The highest position attained either before or since then was sixth place, in1926/27, 1958/59 and 1972/73.

'Big' Jim Barrett, a loyal stalwart who played 467 league and cup matches from 1925 until 1939. But, by contrast, his international career was among the briefest possible. On his debut, Jim lasted just four minutes for England against Northern Ireland in 1929 before

injury struck and he never played for his country again.

Boleyn Ground, the home of the Hammers since 1904. The first game played there, a Southern League match on September 2, saw Hammers emphatically beat arch rivals Millwall 3-0.

Browning Road, East Ham, where Hammers played in 1896/97 after moving from Hermit Road.

Boyce, the midfield dynamo who was the hero of Hammers' FA Cup glory trail in 1964, scoring twice in the epic semi-final win over mighty Manchester United and then the last-minute winner in the Final against Preston North End. 'Ticker' Boyce had served the club as player, coach and chief scout for 37 years before his departure in November 1995.

Brooking, one of the most stylish players to ever pull on a West Ham or England shirt. Midfield maestro Trevor is one of the club's true all-time greats, a fine ambassador for the game as a whole, who 635 senior appearances before retiring in 1984 to take up a successful TV and radio broadcasting career.

'Budgie', the nickname for Johnny Byrne, one of the finest strikers to grace the claret and blue, who cost a British record £65,000 when he signed from Crystal Palace in March 1962.

Bubbles, the title of Hammers' famous anthem which became known world-wide when it rang out around Wembley in 1923. The song was named after a local schoolboy player, 'Bubbles' Murray, who had curly hair and inspired the song 'I'm Forever Blowing Bubbles' among spectators at local schoolboy matches. He bore a striking resemblance to the boy featured in the Pears soap advertisement at that time, illustrated by the famous painting by French artist Millais.

Ronnie Boyce celebrates his last minute headed winner in the 1964 FA Cup Final.

The song was written by American composer James Brockman, who died in 1967.

is for *Cearns*, the family of builders who constructed the West Stand at the Boleyn Ground in 1925. Four generations of the family went on to serve on the club's board of directors: Chairman W.J. Cearns, who died in 1950, was succeeded onto the board by his sons, Will, Len and Brian, while in 1990 Len's son, Martin, became the club's youngest chairman at the age of 44. He became vice-chairman in 1992, handing 'the chair' to Terry Brown.

Charles, the local-born left-back became the first black player to play for the club when he made his

debut in 1963. John, or 'Charlo' as he was known, also led Hammers to victory in the 1963 FA Youth Cup Final. John paved the way for several more coloured players to break through into the first team in the late 60s and early 70s, including his younger brother Clive, Clyde Best and Ade Coker.

Charity Shield, the annual league champions v. FA Cup winners clash that has featured Hammers on three occasions. We shared the shield with Liverpool after a 2-2 draw at Anfield in 1964, but lost at Wembley to Derby County in 1975 and Liverpool in 1980.

Claret and Blue, the colours of West Ham United.

Chicken Run, the popular, old wooden stand, with its corrugated iron roof, that housed the most vocal of Hammers' supporters before it was demolished in 1968 to make way for the East Stand.

Cottee became the club's record transfer sale when he joined Everton for a British record £2.05 million in July 1988. After six full seasons at Goodison, Tony returned to lead the Hammers' attack again in September 1994.

D is for **Dagenham Motors**, who became new club sponsors in 1992, signing a five-year agreement.

Dear, who set an English First Division record when he scored five times against West Bromwich Albion in the

Above: Alan Devonshire, a great player and a real bargain.
Left: Jimmy Greaves maintained his scoring debut record.
Below: Julian Dicks, a cult hero at Upton Park.

space of just 20 minutes (either side of half-time) on April 16, 1965.

Debuts, one of the most notable being Jimmy Greaves' two-goal strike on his Hammers' bow in the mud at Manchester City in March 1970. The goalscoring legend was way past his best by the time he arrived at Upton Park in the part-exchange deal that took Martin Peters to Tottenham but 'Greavsie's' performance at Maine Road maintained his record of having scored on every debut throughout his illustrious career.

Devonshire, one of the all-time bargain buys when he signed from non-league Southall for just £5,000 in 1976. One of the most talented and creative players in the British game, 'Dev' went on to make 446 first team appearances.

Dick, fourth in the list of West Ham's all-time leading goalscorers. John netted 153 goals in 326 league appearances, including a career best 21 in the 1957/58 Second Division promotion campaign.

Dicks, the cult hero of the modern-day fans. Julian's undoubted ability as one of the most talented left-backs in the country is harshly overshadowed by his record of disciplinary problems.

Kvasnak, of Czech team Spartak Prague, bemoans his luck after his overhead kick flew wide. Hammers breathing a sigh of relief are, left to right, Bobby Moore, John Bond, Martin Peters, Ken Brown, Jim Standen and Ronnie Boyce. Sissons scored the vital goal in this 1965 ECWC second round, second leg tie which ended 2-1 to the Czechs, but with Hammers going through on aggregate. Note the square goalposts.

E is for *Europe*, which West Ham conquered so gloriously in May 1965, when we defeated TSV Munich of West Germany 2-0 in front of 100,000 fans at Wembley Stadium. The achievement of that night, acclaimed throughout the world as a performance as near perfect as possible, tends to overshadow the fact that Hammers did very well to also reach the semi-finals in defence of their title the following season. They went all the way to the Final of the European Cup Winners' Cup for a second time in 1976, losing to Anderlecht of Belgium, 4-2, in Brussels. Our last involvement in Europe came in 1981, when the talented Russian side Dynamo Tbilisi knocked us out in the third round of the ECWC.

East Stand, the two-tier construction that replaced the old Chicken Run was officially opened on January 4, 1969, by Charlie Paynter, although fans were previously admitted to the lower, terraced, area on November 2, 1968.

Eight-nil the Hammers' record league win, achieved against Sunderland in the First Division on October 19, 1968, and in the Second Division against Rotherham United on March 8, 1958.

F is for *FA Cup*, the trophy Hammers have lifted three times – in 1964, 1975 and 1980. We were, however, the first-ever beaten finalists at Wembley, losing 2-0 to Bolton Wanderers in 1923. Billy Bonds was skipper of both the 1975 and 1980 winning teams.

Fenton, who made 163 league appearances as a player before succeeding Charlie Paynter as manager in 1950. Ted guided the team back to the First Division, after an absence of 26 years, as Second Division champions in 1958.

FA Youth Cup, a trophy West Ham have won twice – in 1963 and 1981, beating Liverpool and Spurs respectively, although we were losing finalists in 1957 (to Manchester United), 1959 (Blackburn Rovers) and 1975 (Ipswich Town).

Floodlights, which were first installed at Upton Park in 1953. The first game under lights was a 2-1 victory over Spurs on April 16. The first floodlit league match was against Bury on March 19, 1956.

Footballer of the Year, a distinguished award won by Bobby Moore in 1964.

Football League. Hammers were elected to Division Two in 1919, and the first league game was at home against Lincoln City on August 30 that year. It ended 1-1. Our opening away fixture resulted in a 7-0 defeat at Barnsley on September 1.

Foreign opposition. The first overseas visitors to Upton Park were Dutch side Haarlem, who were beaten 4-2 on December 27, 1921. Our first-ever game on the continent came the previous February, a 4-0 victory over Madrid in Spain.

G is for ***goalkeepers***, the most expensive in the world being Phil Parkes, when John Lyall signed him from Queens Park Rangers in February 1979 for £565,000. 'Parkesy' made 344 league appearances for Hammers and was still a First Division regular at the age of 39. Bobby Ferguson had previously been a British record buy when Ron Greenwood signed him from Kilmarnock for £65,000 in 1967. But no 'keeper served the club longer than Ernie Gregory, who joined the groundstaff in 1936 and played and coached at Upton Park for a further 50 years. He made 406 league and cup appearances.

Goulden, one of the all-time greats. Len was capped 20 times by England.

Greenwood, a footballing purist who came from Arsenal to manage Hammers in 1961. Within four years Ron's exciting brand of open, attacking football, with the emphasis always on skill, led to glory in the 1964 FA Cup and 1965 European Cup Winners' Cup Finals. He vacated the manager's seat at Upton Park in 1977 to become manager of England.

Green Street, the road in East Ham that houses the Boleyn Ground. Contrary to popular belief, the ground is actually in East Ham and not Upton Park.

H is for ***Hammers***, the nickname of West Ham United. The crossed hammers crest emanates from West Ham's

A formal gathering of West Ham and England personalities, left to right: Don Howe, Bobby Robson, Geoff Hurst, John Lyall, Trevor Brooking and Ron Greenwood.

Stairway of stars...Ted Fenton with skipper Harry Kinsell (with ball) and trainer Billy Moore, looks up to: Jimmy Andrews, Ken Brown, Tommy Dixon, Andy Malcolm, Dave Sexton, Doug Bing, George Taylor and Les Bennett. Can anyone name the player top right?

Crowning glory...Bobby Moore inspects the Jules Rimet Trophy after leading England to their epic 4-2 victory over West Germany in the 1966 World Cup Final at Wembley.

predecessors, the Thames Ironworks, where hammers were prominent factory tools.

Hammer of the Year, the award voted for each season by supporters. Trevor Brooking is the only player to have won it five times.

Hat-tricks. The most notable was that scored by central defender Alvin Martin who scored against three DIFFERENT 'keepers when Newcastle United visited on April 21, 1986. The unlucky trio were: Martin Thomas, Chris Hedworth and Peter Beardsley. However, in 1948, West ham had been on the receiving end of the same rare feat, when Lincoln's Jack Dodds scored past Ernie Gregory, Tommy Moroney and George Dick.

Hermit Road, Canning Town, the home of Thames Ironworks for several games in 1896, when matches were played under electric lights mounted on poles.

Hills, Arnold, the founder of Thames Ironworks and West Ham United. His great-grandson, Charles Warner, was elected to the board in November 1988.

Hurst, the heroic hat-trick hitter for England in the 1966 World Cup Final. Geoff also won cup-winners' medals with the Hammers in 1964 and 1965 and firmly established as one of the club's all-time leading goalscorers. Only Vic Watson has scored more than Geoff's 248 league and cup goals in 499 appearances.

Hat-trick hero Alvin Martin in action during the 1980 FA Cup Final victory over Arsenal.

I is for *internationals.* Bobby Moore is by far the most capped Hammer to represent his country, winning 108 full caps for England – a record bettered only by goalkeeper Peter Shilton. In all, West Ham have provided 22 full internationals for England, the last being Tony Cottee in April 1988.

Irons, West Ham's alternative nickname.

J is for *Jones*, who became the first West Ham player to be capped for his country. Welsh international William played against England and Scotland in 1902.

K is for *Kay*, one of the first West Ham players to make a success of management. In his first season as skipper, George led Hammers to promotion and the 1923 FA Cup Final. He also became the first to play more than 200 league games for the club. Kay later guided Liverpool to the First Division title as manager in 1947.

Keeble, Vic, who scored 19 vital goals in a potent twin spearhead with Johnny Dick that clinched the Second Division championship in 1958.

King, a former player and secretary, became the first manager of West Ham United in 1901. E.S. – or 'Syd' – King led the team out at the 1923 FA Cup Final as well as guiding them out of the Second Division that same season. He also embraced the era in which Hammers turned professional (1919) but he was devastated by the club's relegation in 1931. Soon after being dismissed by the board in 1933, he committed suicide.

Kitchen, George, who has the distinction of being the only goalkeeper to score for West Ham – a penalty against Swindon Town in 1905/06!

GALLAHER'S CIGARETTES

GEORGE KITCHEN, WEST HAM UNITED, 1909-10

L is for **Lampard**, assistant to manager Harry Redknapp whose haul of 660 league and cup appearances between 1967 and 1985 is surpassed only by Billy Bonds.

Lyall, John, who spent 34 loyal years at Upton Park as player, office clerk, coach and then manager before he was sacked after the team's relegation from the old First Division in 1989. Strongly influenced by his mentor, Ron Greenwood, he maintained the club's tradition for playing open, attacking football and was team manager for both the 1975 and 1980 FA Cup triumphs.

League Cup, a competition in which Hammers have a very respectable record. Although we have yet to lift the Football League Cup, in any of its various guises since its inception in 1960, we were losers in the two-leg final against West Bromwich Albion in 1966 and Liverpool in 1981 (after a replay), and reached the semi-finals in 1967, 1972, 1989 and 1990.

Live TV game. The first at Upton Park was a floodlit friendly, in 1955, between West Ham and Holland Sports, screened by the BBC. It was not a memorable occasion for the TV crew, however, as the game ended goalless! The club pulled off a first when, in March 1955, BBC cameras were also present to capture the signing of forward Billy Dare from Brentford by manager Ted Fenton, screened on the *Sportsview* programme.

 is for **Managing Director**. The club appointed its first full-time executive from the board in November 1991, when Peter Storrie became M.D.

Match of the Day. West Ham were featured in the first ever colour screening of a league

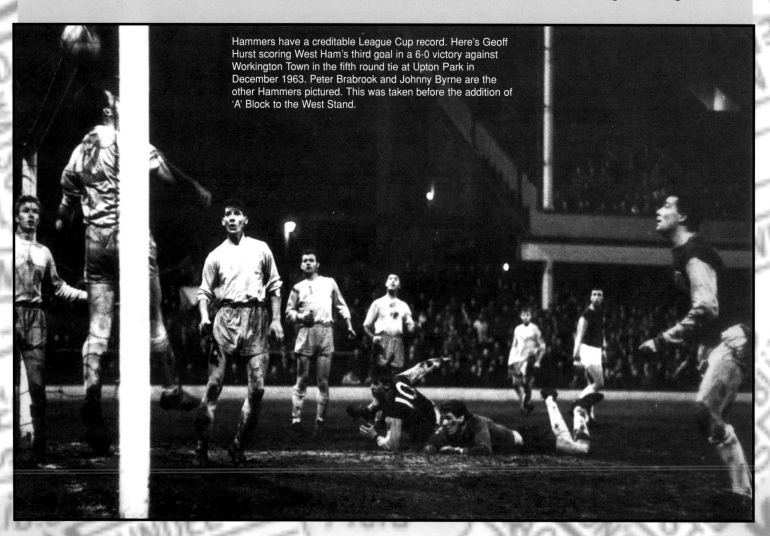

Hammers have a creditable League Cup record. Here's Geoff Hurst scoring West Ham's third goal in a 6-0 victory against Workington Town in the fifth round tie at Upton Park in December 1963. Peter Brabrook and Johnny Byrne are the other Hammers pictured. This was taken before the addition of 'A' Block to the West Stand.

game, at Liverpool in 1969.

Moore, acclaimed by most people as the greatest West Ham player of all. Bobby made his debut against Manchester United in 1958 and immediately established himself as an accomplished defender way beyond his tender years. 'Mooro' skippered Hammers to FA Cup glory in 1964 – the start of a triumphant hat-trick of Wembley victories that also included the 1965 European Cup Winners' Cup and the 1966 World Cup. A legend of world football, he made 544 league and 98 cup appearances for West Ham before moving to Fulham in 1974. A year later he was back at Wembley, but had to settle for a losers' medal against his former club. The whole of football mourned his untimely death, at the age of 51, on February 24, 1993.

McAvennie, one of the most popular and charismatic players to wear the claret and blue. He scored 26 goals in the club's best-ever league campaign, 1985/86 – the first to net more than 25 in one league season since Bryan 'Pop' Robson in 1972/73.

Memorial Grounds, Canning Town, the first home of West Ham United after their name changed from Thames Ironworks in 1900.

is for **Newham**, the London borough council where Hammers are situated.
North Bank, the terraced stand populated by the most vocal of Hammers' support for many years. Originally uncovered, its roof was installed in the summer of 1961. But that end of the ground was demolished in the summer of 1994 to make way for the new Centenary Stand.

John Lyall welcomes his world record signing Phil Parkes.

is for **O.B.E.**, the Queen's award received by Bobby Moore, for his services to football, in February 1967.

Oldest player. Billy Bonds holds the record for West Ham, making his final appearance at Southampton on April 30, 1988, aged 41 years and 226 days. He just pipped 1930s defender and another former captain, Charlie Bicknell, who was aged 41 years and 59 days old when he played his final match for the club against Leicester City on January 4, 1947.

is for **Parkes**, the goalkeeper Hammers paid Queens Park Rangers a world record £565,000 for in February 1979.

Paynter, who signed as an amateur player in 1900, was appointed reserve team trainer four years later and was promoted to first team duties in 1912. Taking over as manager from Syd King in 1932, in all Charlie completed 50 years service with the club.

Peters, the third member of the famous 1966 World Cup trio who made 302 league appearances but, most admirably, scored 81 goals – a remarkable ratio for a midfield player. Martin, who made so many other goals for teammate Geoff Hurst, was also a member of the 1965 ECWC-winning team. He moved to Spurs in a record £200,000 deal in March 1970.

Premier League, the name the FA adopted to succeed the old First Division. Hammers' first fixture in the newly-named top division was at home to Wimbledon on August 14, 1993. New signing from Glasgow Rangers, Dale

goal in the Premier League, at Coventry City a week later.

Puddefoot. West Ham striker Syd Puddefoot cost Falkirk a world record £5,000 fee in 1921.

Q is for *Queen's Honours List.* After Bobby Moore was awarded the O.B.E. in 1967, there were subsequent M.B.E. awards for Martin Peters (1978) Trevor Brooking (1981) and Billy Bonds (1988). Former West Ham and England manager Ron Greenwood received the C.B.E. in 1981.

Quinn. Northern Ireland international striker Jimmy Quinn is the only player, whose surname begins with the letter 'Q', who has ever played first team football for Hammers!

R is for *Redknapp*, the current West Ham manager. A product of Hammers' thriving youth policy in the mid-60s, Eastender Harry made 149 first team appearances between 1965 and 1972 before he ventured into management. After nine years in charge at Bournemouth, 'H' returned to Upton Park as assistant to Billy Bonds in August 1992. Between them, they steered Hammers back to the top flight that season. Redknapp stepped up to become the new number one when 'Bonzo' quit in August 1994.

1964, and Hammers' first FA Cup success. Manager Ron Greenwood joins the players on the pitch after our 3-2 win over Preston North End.

Jim Standen makes a flying save against Liverpool, watched by (left to right): Eddie Bovington, Ian St. John, Martin Peters, Eddie Presland, Bobby Moore and Chris Lawler.

Record signing. Hammers' most expensive signing is Don Hutchison, whom Harry Redknapp bought from Liverpool for £1.5 million in August 1994.

Robson. Several players of this surname have played for West Ham but the best known is Geordie Bryan 'Pop' Robson, a renowned goalscorer who enjoyed two spells in East London during the 70s. His 28 First Division league goals in 1972/73 have not been bettered since then.

Ruffell, another prolific forward who stands up there among the greatest goalscorers, having hit 159 in 505 league outings between 1921 and 1937. Not bad for a winger! Indeed, Jimmy

currently stands third in the club's all-time scorers' list.

 is for **Sealey**, the two-goal hero of the 1965 ECWC triumph. The bustling winger was the pride of London after his double sunk TSV Munich 1860, but the year ended in misery when he broke his leg in a freak training ground accident.

Shea, Danny, became the most expensive player in Britain when, in 1913, West Ham sold him to Blackburn Rovers for £2,000.

Bryan 'Pop' Robson

Sissons, who became, at 19, the youngest player to score in an FA Cup Final at Wembley. John's opener set Hammers on their way to a 3-2 victory over Preston North End in May 1964.

Six goal haul – the personal, record-breaking tally achieved in one game by both Vic Watson and Geoff Hurst. Watson scored six in a 8-2 victory over Leeds United on February 9, 1929, while Hurst equalled that club record in the 8-0 win over Sunderland on October 19, 1968.

Southern League, the competition Thames Ironworks entered and competed in from 1898 until 1915.

South Bank, the terraced Castle Street end of the ground. Originally an earthen mound edged with timbers to make rough terracing, it was the first end to be covered, adopting the old West Stand roof in 1925. It was replaced in March 1994 by the new, two-tier South Stand named after Bobby Moore.

Standen, Jim, who won a County Championship winners' medal with Worcestershire Cricket Club AND an FA Cup winners' medal with Hammers, in addition to taking 64 wickets at an average of 13 runs, in 1964.

Substitute. The first Hammer to be used as a substitute was Peter Bennett, who replaced Jack Burkett at Leeds on

Don Hutchison became West Ham's new record signing when he joined us from Liverpool in August 1994 for £1.5 million.

August 28, 1965. History was made again on August 15, 1987, in the home game against Queens Park Rangers, when Alan Dickens and Gary Strodder were the first double substitutes. The first goalkeeper to be named as a substitute for Hammers was Phil Parkes, at Newcastle, on May 7, 1988, although he did not play.

T is for **Taylor**, Alan, who hit the headlines during our successful FA Cup run of 1975, scoring both goals in the quarter-final win at Arsenal, again in the semi-final replay victory over Ipswich Town and then, sensationally, in the Final itself against Fulham.

Ten-nil, the record-breaking Milk Cup thrashing Hammers inflicted upon Bury in the second round (second leg) of the League Cup competition on October 25, 1983.

Thames Ironworks, the forebears of West Ham United. Formed in 1895 by workers in the old ship-building company on the banks of the Thames, they played friendly matches until becoming professional and entering the Southern League in 1898.

Testimonials. Only two players have been awarded

Ham – Billy Bonds and Alvin Martin were both being rewarded for more than 20 years loyal service.

U is for *Upton Park*, the home of the Hammers! *United States of America*, where Hammers made history on April 19, 1967, becoming the first English team to play on a full size pitch completely under cover. The match was against Spanish giants Real of Madrid in the Houston Astrodome, Texas.

is for *Van Der Elst*, whose performance for Anderlecht in the 1976 ECWC Final promoted John Lyall to sign the Belgian international for West Ham in 1981.

V *V1*, the German flying bomb that struck the south-west corner of the Boleyn Ground and caused such damage in August 1944. Hammers had to play their next nine matches away from home – and won them all! But then lost their first match back at the Boleyn, to Spurs!

W is for *Walker*, Dick, who served the Hammers well in more than 300 games between 1934 and 1953. Albert Walker (no relation) spent 34 years with the

club as player and coach before and after world war two.

War Cup, which Hammers won in 1940, the only time the competition was not regionalised. Hammers beat Blackburn Rovers 1-0 with a Sam Small goal. The trophy still stands proudly in the Upton Park boardroom.

Watson, Vic, is West Ham's all-time record goalscorer, with a massive 326 league and cup goals to his credit between 1921 and 1935.

V. WATSON
'WEST HAM UNITED'

Webb, George, who was the first Hammer to be capped for England at full international level, in 1911.

West Stand, the first and biggest stand at Upton Park, opened in 1925. Built with the proceeds from the 1923 FA Cup run, at the time it was the biggest football stand at an English league ground. The lower tier terracing was converted to seats in the summer of 1981.

World Cup. The last Hammer to appear in the finals was Alvin Martin, who played for

England in a 3-0 win against Paraguay in Mexico in 1986.

X is for *X-rated*. The 'Hammer Horror Show' took place on Boxing Day, 1963, when West Ham lost at home to Blackburn Rovers by a record 8-2 margin . . . and then, typically, won the return match, two days later, 3-1!

Y is for *Yews*, Tommy, of whom Charlie Paynter once said: 'He could pick a fly off Vic Watson's eyebrows, with his crosses'. In 332 league matches for Hammers, the winger scored 51 goals and made countless others.

Z is for *Zaragoza, Real*, the Spanish team, who were beaten by West Ham in the semi-final of the 1965 ECWC tournament.

Zabrze, Gornik, the Polish opposition Hammers defeated to win the American International Soccer League, held in New York in the summer of 1963.